MENTAL RETARDATION:
OCCASIONAL PAPERS 2, 3 & 4

MENTAL RETARDATION: OCCASIONAL PAPERS 2, 3 & 4

2 — **The Quality of Survival**

KENNETH S. HOLT, MD, FRCP, DCH

3 — **The Need for Long-term Care**

SHEILA HEWETT, BA, PhD

4 — **Growing Up in Hospital**

ELSPETH STEPHEN, MA, DipEd
and
JEAN ROBERTSON, BSc, DipPsychol

Published for the Institute for Research into Mental Retardation

LONDON: BUTTERWORTHS

ENGLAND: BUTTERWORTH & CO. (PUBLISHERS) LTD.
                LONDON: 88 Kingsway, WC2B 6AB

AUSTRALIA: BUTTERWORTHS PTY. LTD.
                SYDNEY: 586 Pacific Highway, 2067
                MELBOURNE: 343 Little Collins Street, 3000
                BRISBANE: 240 Queen Street, 4000

CANADA: BUTTERWORTH & CO. (CANADA) LTD.
                TORONTO: 14 Curity Avenue, 374

NEW ZEALAND: BUTTERWORTHS OF NEW ZEALAND LTD.
                WELLINGTON: 26–28 Waring Taylor Street, 1

SOUTH AFRICA: BUTTERWORTH & CO. (SOUTH AFRICA) (PTY) LTD.
                DURBAN: 152–154 Gale Street

Suggested UDC Number: 616·899: 362·3

ISBN: 0 407 26830 8

Printed offset in Great Britain by
The Camelot Press Ltd, London and Southampton

Contents

Foreword

The three papers in this volume explore some facets of the immense social changes which have taken place during the past century. They are published under the auspices of the Institute for Research into Mental Retardation and all illuminate some aspect of the social background against which the problem of mental handicap develops. It is significant that some of the institutions for the mentally retarded which have been so heavily criticized of late have just celebrated their centenary whilst others are older. It is not surprising in view of this fact that Pauline Morris should have found conditions in some such hospitals 'positively Dickensian', nor that Elspeth Stephen and Jean Robertson in reporting their efforts to improve the hospital environment should feel that they only partially succeeded in making the ward comfortable and homelike.

Dr. Holt's paper presents much of the essential background which enables current problems of mental handicap to be seen in perspective. He summarizes trends in mother and child health showing the dramatic improvement since the beginning of this century in the 'quantity' of survival, that is, the remarkable drop in the infantile mortality rate. Hence the title of his contribution – 'The quality of survival'. If mere quantity is considered alone, it is worth remarking that Britain is only tenth by this standard of international competition. Some such as Sweden do conspicuously better. Is this due to a more even distribution of wealth and availability of essential services? Pasamanick and Knobloch's thesis of a continuum of reproductive casualty seems amply borne out by the findings of the Perinatal Mortality Survey and subsequent cohort studies by Professor Butler and his colleagues, which are quoted by Dr. Holt. If infant mortality could be reduced to the level of that in Sweden or to that in Social Class I, there would be a great reduction not only in infant deaths but also in infant morbidity including brain damage and mental handicap.

As Dr. Holt points out, misunderstanding of Darwin's findings and a crude application of the concept of 'survival of the fittest' has led some to question the effect of the humanitarian approach and efforts to promote survival of the handicapped. All the evidence suggests that an all-out effort to improve maternal health and render the environment in which the child grows up more satisfactory will greatly reduce the numbers of the handicapped.

Despite these efforts there is at the present time and there will continue to be for the foreseeable future a very large number of families with handicapped members who are in need of help and advice. Holt argues, as did Penrose, that the provision of this service is a useful moral exercise for society. It is indeed gratifying in the light of criticism so often levelled at the young generation, to see the cheerful enthusiasm with which young volunteers tackle the care of the most severely handicapped children and adults.

The present emphasis in the care of the mentally retarded is on 'normalization'. This word has a fine ring to it but it could be used simply as an excuse for failure to provide services. The Education Act, 1970, represents a big step in the direction of normal provision and all children now have a right to education, but Sheila Hewett gives examples of children who had to be admitted to hospital because there was no suitable daytime provision. There is no doubt that if the money is available and the community services are provided, the need for hospital admission can be very greatly reduced. However, at present very many families are left with the full-time care of a handicapped member. This is particularly true of adults but it is also true of a minority of children with multiple handicap who are rejected by schools.

Dr. Holt's message is that given the necessary effort the quality of survival can be enhanced. Dr. Hewett shows that for those who, despite such improvements, are still handicapped the need for institutional care can be greatly reduced if community services are provided. Miss Stephen and Miss Robertson demonstrate that institutions can be made better places in which to live and that the social dependence of their inmates can be reduced. All of this implies an ambitious programme and drastic reappraisal by society of available resources.

BRIAN KIRMAN, MD, DPM, FRCPsych
Consultant Psychiatrist
Queen Mary's Hospital for Children
Carshalton, Surrey

2 – The Quality of Survival

Kenneth S. Holt, MD, FRCP, DCH

Director, The Wolfson Centre and
Department of Developmental Paediatrics
Institute of Child Health, University of London

Contents

Preface

I have thought about the problems of the mentally subnormal for many years, and, after writing the Milroy Lectures, I have given even more attention to the subject. Our attitudes towards the subnormal appear to reflect so many deep values of life itself, and are a measure of our personal opinions. It seemed appropriate, therefore, that I should add the first short chapter which summarizes some of my current thoughts on the subject.

KENNETH S. HOLT

Mental Subnormality and Human Dignity

The word 'subnormal' is belittling and degrading. The phrase 'mentally subnormal' is especially degrading because we regard mental attributes so highly. Now that the people of many countries enjoy excellent health and take for granted the survival for life of all their children, they increasingly demand that this survival be of the highest quality. Can there then be a place for the mentally subnormal? Now that people accept the results of modern technology, they find that the pattern of their lives is more complex and the pace is quicker, and this places more demands upon their skills and abilities. Can there then be a place for the less able, the mentally subnormal?

This question has always existed and required answers from both individuals and society, but never before has the question been so imperative and the answers so elusive. The great medical advances of recent decades which give most of us healthy long lives, have led also to the survival of many handicapped individuals who in earlier years would have 'enjoyed nature's release' through pneumonia. This phrase flows readily because the sentiments are familiar and acceptable to us. In using the words 'enjoyed nature's release' we are, in fact, imparting a wish fulfilment to the statement. I believe that in the past the vast majority of people were thankful when nature took its course and a severely handicapped person died. They accepted that there were times when it was better for severely handicapped individuals to be 'mercifully released' rather than continue their suffering and discomfort. It was always difficult to know whether these feelings stemmed from a genuine concern for the individual or arose as a consequence of increasing difficulty for those caring for the person, or even because they really did consider that there was no place for the mentally subnormal.

Powerful antibiotics enable us to control and even to reverse nature's course, so we can no longer evade facing these difficult questions as we might have done in the past.

There is not one single question to which we must find answers, but several. The principal issues appear to be as follows.

(1)   Is there ever a time when it is preferable for the severely handicapped person to die for their own sake? How do we tell? How should they die? Who should decide?

(2)   Is there ever a time when it is preferable for a severely handicapped person to die for the sake of others or because there is no care available? Can we decide limits for the amount of care available?

5

(3)   Is there ever a time when it is preferable for a severely handicapped person to die in order to promote a better quality of survival? Do we know what quality of survival we want?

(4)   Is there ever a time when it is preferable for a severely handicapped person to die because we have created a society which is ill-fitted for him and we cannot find any other solution?

Upon meeting a severely subnormal person, it is an almost instinctive action to imagine oneself in their situation and to try to see the world as they see it. We then feel relieved because we are not so afflicted. In consequence, however, we may estimate incorrectly their distress, suffering and misery, and, as we realize our inaccuracy, may come to doubt whether we can accurately judge when life becomes too much for them. If we personally have doubts about our ability to make an accurate assessment in these situations, is it likely that anyone else will be able to do so? Realization of all our limitations in these circumstances might bring with it understanding that every individual's comfort and sense of well-being depends to a large extent upon the reactions of others. The greatest proof of this is the wonderful expression on the face of a subnormal child who is appreciated for himself. If we acknowledge that we cannot accurately judge the level of tolerance of life of others, especially of the mentally subnormal, then perhaps we might use our energies more effectively by finding ways to improve their tolerance of life. This is today's need. We are living in the present, and not yet in a scientific Utopia. Research must continue to strive to find causes, preventions and cures, but with research for the future must be associated sound care for those living in the present. This I believe to be a profoundly important precept and one which I pursue in my professional work.

Should it be accepted that there are circumstances in which, for their own sake, severely mentally subnormal persons are better not continuing the struggle with life, then how should they die? Should this be left to chance: for 'nature to take its course'? Infections may come along and antibiotics can be withheld. Everyone who has witnessed such an end will testify that death can be prolonged and uncomfortable. Having reached, by careful thought and reasoning, the conclusion that a 'merciful release' is desirable, many feel that it is most logical and compassionate to make such an end comfortable and speedy. In fact, it would be dignified to do so (Ritchie-Calder, 1971). However, until such policies are made and accepted, should we not proceed to make their lives as personally satisfying and tolerable as possible?

Of the four groups of questions posed earlier the issues just discussed are probably the most important and most urgently in need of solution. The answers to all the other questions are influenced by economic considerations in the widest sense. If we consider that there may be a time when it is preferable for a severely handicapped person to die rather than continue to live, because of the strain upon others or because there is no care available, then we are admitting that we cannot provide that care and do not wish to divert resources from other areas to make it possible. There will be occasions, such as times of national disaster, when groups are in such dire circumstances that this situation pertains, but in present-day conditions it would be difficult to consider terminating life because of the total unavailability of care. Some may argue that there is no justification for expending energies in situations from which there can be no return, and so not make care available. But are we really happy to judge these issues at a basic material level? And even if we were, who is to be the evaluator? To expend resources for care in these circumstances may not be economically sound, yet we turn away from an economic solution. Provision of care can be justified on the basis of compassion and humanitarianism, and some suggest that we should welcome all opportunities to exercise these feelings because nowadays such chances occur all too seldom (Dybwad, 1969). Also, there are indications that, in an increasingly affluent society, the young people are seeking such opportunities.

Devotion and compassion are admirable attributes which add to the quality of life. Those who seek a higher quality of life only in intellectual and material terms may lose these other valuable contributions to such quality. It would seem that as a society we will wish to provide care for our mentally subnormal and so preserve these qualities of devotion and compassion, but there will always be some individuals whose resources are more than fully stretched by close proximity to problems of care, and who will continue to find relief in 'nature's release'.

The long-standing proposition that the quality of survival can be promoted by eradication of the subnormal does not gain ground. Eradication of the subnormal in one generation will not prevent the occurrence of subnormality in future generations. Eradication of the most subnormal will fractionally raise the average performance of the group, but lead in turn to the successive eradication of the next lowest group in order to achieve even better results — and then where would it all end? There is a need to view this situation from a biological standpoint. We have developed as a biological species because of our variability. This possibility for genetic variation is essential for our continued development and should be preserved (Dobzhansky, 1966).

The fourth group of questions acknowledge that life in present-day society is ill-suited for the mentally subnormal. The contrast between the good health and prospects for the mass of people and the limitations of the subnormal is greater now than ever before. Also, life is faster and more complex. Modern transport and methods of communication are just two areas where these difficulties are obvious. For example, using a telephone with sometimes six, seven or even eight numbers in the code is beyond the capability of many of the subnormal. Thus, in creating a more sophisticated and complex world we have made life more difficult for the mentally subnormal. Have we made it so very difficult that they are no longer acceptable? It would seem strange if we could not bring ourselves to apply the knowledge and skill which has created modern society to find ways to enable the subnormal to be part of and to participate in

7

that society. Yet at times it appears that such application is low down on the priority lists.

If we fail to find solutions, we fail not because of our lack of skill and resources, but because of our attitudes towards the subnormal, and this is the fundamental question we have to face. Do we personally reject the subnormal? Do we collectively reject the subnormal? In so doing we lose some of the qualities which contribute to the value of life — qualities which would help us to lead fuller lives ourselves and with one another. In rejecting the subnormal we could lose an opportunity to enhance human dignity.

So far, I have written about severe mental subnormality and in such a way as to suggest that it is a fixed condition. This is not so: mental subnormality is not static. All measures of mental subnormality are comparative and its severity is proportional to limitations of the individual to meet the requirements of society. On the one hand the individual has to be helped to meet the demands of his environment, and on the other hand his environment has to be modified to reduce the discrepancy. Much more could be done in both these areas if we wished. To do so will increase our pride in caring and showing compassion, and as we ourselves in turn leave this life we might do so with greater dignity, having helped to perpetuate the spirit of compassion. I believe this is what William James had in mind when he wrote that the greatest purpose in life is to spend it for something which outlasts it (James, 1902).

Introduction to the Milroy Lectures on the Quality of Survival

It is my privilege this year (1969) to be the Milroy lecturer here at the Royal College of Physicians under the bequest of Gavin Milroy. He made this bequest to the College for the establishment of a few lectures every year on the subject of state medicine and public hygiene. He put forward several suggestions about the lectures for consideration by the Council, writing as follows:

> 'my only desire being how most usefully to promote the advancement of medical science along with the interests of philanthropic benevolence and social welfare.'

It is interesting that he used the term medical science at a time when pasteurization (L. Pasteur, 1864) and anaesthesia (C. W. Long, removed tumour under ether 1842) were barely accepted discoveries, and the possibility of electronic aids for diagnosis and antibiotics for treatment were inconceivable. It is also interesting to note that he realized that the advancement of medicine must be linked with science and, equally, with benevolence and welfare.

As this year's Milroy lecturer, I have taken these words of Gavin Milroy in my consideration of that vital aspect of child health, which is survival. The application of Gavin Milroy's ideas (as expressed in the above sentence) to child health, seems particularly appropriate at this time because this branch of medicine is changing and advancing greatly, and is entering upon a period when child health, education and welfare will need to be closely connected, just as Milroy implied.

That Milroy conceived this connection 100 years ago is remarkable. Circumstances were very different from the present time when he was practising in late Victorian England. The picture at that time has been vividly described by Neale in the Heath Clark lectures (1964). Survival from death was all important because many mothers and babies did not survive. Maternal mortality was very high until the middle of the nineteenth century, when the teachings of Semmelweis spread; but even then, rates of 12–20 per 1,000 total births were recorded. The infant mortality rate was approximately 150 per 1,000 live births (*Figure 2.1*). Women were apprehensive about childbirth and considered

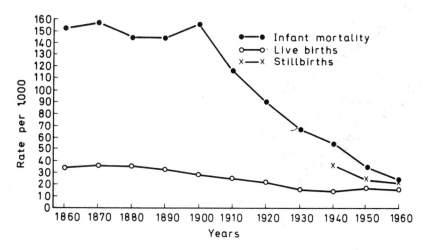

Figure 2.1. Child health from 1860 to 1960: infant mortality, live birth and stillbirth rates (data from Registrar General, 1965)

themselves lucky when they and their children survived. Many families had lost children and mothers of their own, and many more knew families well who had suffered in this way — a state of affairs so appalling compared with the present that one wonders how they tolerated it. However, it is necessary for us to see it as only one of many appalling facts of life of the second half of the nineteenth century.

Infections of all kinds were prevalent and uncontrolled. Cholera epidemics were only just being brought under control in the capital city; diphtheria, pneumonia, meningitis and tuberculosis took a heavy toll of life. Jonathan Hutchinson was writing about the clinical features of syphilitic infection in children (Hutchinson, 1861), and the possibility that tuberculosis was due to an infectious agent was just being described (Villemin, 1868). Relatively little was known about nutrition, and malnutrition was common particularly in the poorer classes. Against this background of the ravages of infections and malnutrition, there were many who misinterpreted the teachings of Darwin (1859) and argued fiercely the advantages of a high mortality rate as favouring the survival of the fittest; they tried to deter pioneers of public health, such as our first Registrar General, William Farr, from their efforts to promote survival.

The value of life of the working class was cheap in those days. Children were sent to work in appalling conditions at an early age, and were even sent to prison or deported for trivial reasons. Compulsory education was not brought in until 1876 and then only up to 10 years of age. Another 23 years elapsed before the age was extended to 12 years, in 1899.

How amazing it is to remember the great achievements which this ill-favoured era had seen. Amongst the great personalities of this period were Disraeli and Livingstone, and they witnessed great activity in all parts of the Empire. The Suez Canal shares were acquired in 1875, and the Queen was declared Empress of India in 1877. Typewriters appeared in 1874, the telephone in 1877 and electric light in 1880. Truly this was a period of great development in all fields.

Milroy and his colleagues must have found it very difficult to see their environment in perspective as we see it today. Many of them thought deeply about medical matters, as is evident in many ways, not least of which was Milroy's bequest; they set us an example to consider fearlessly the problems of our own day.

How much happier we present-day parents are to be able to look forward to good health for ourselves and for our children. The marked decline in maternal mortality began between the two world wars and such deaths are now rare (*Figure 2.2*). Infant mortality is one-tenth of that 100 years ago. Not only is it becoming possible to take survival for granted, but poor survival is becoming less acceptable. A high quality of survival is important. Families are limited, and every child is carefully nurtured. Parents who are considering adoption, or the advisability of another pregnancy after the birth of a defective child, often ask paediatricians to guarantee that the baby will be perfect — anything less would be unacceptable.

We are thus entering the era where quality of survival is important. This is already having wide repercussions and, for example, it is probable that the

10

demand for this quality made circumstances appropriate for the introduction and acceptance of the Abortion Act of 1967 (Addison, 1968). Mortality is no longer a measure of our problems, but we are concerned with the problem of inferior quality of survival.

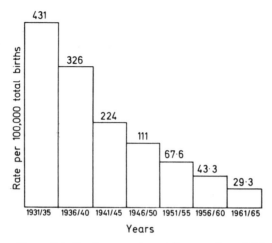

Figure 2.2. Total maternal mortality rate from 1931 to 1965 (data from Registrar General, 1965)

Further consideration of this question of survival seems to fall into three sections. The first concerns the survival for birth, the second the survival at birth for life, and the third the survival of some individuals with help, that is, the handicapped.

Survival Becomes Possible: Conception—Birth

Life begins at the time of conception, and growth and development continue until maturity is reached. Biological maturity occurs after approximately 15 years, but man is unique in that intellectual and social maturation may continue for several years longer. At some time after reaching maturity, reproduction may occur to continue the species. Thereafter the parent organism regresses and dies.

11

The human biological cycle is characterized at the present time by widespread limitation of conception, arrival at biological maturity slightly earlier than in the past (and thereby further increasing the educational, social and cultural problems of this stage) (Tanner, 1962) and marked prolongation of the post-reproductive regression phase. As we are concerned with the quality of survival, we need to consider the implications of each stage of this biological cycle; that is, the quality of those conceived, the rearing of the children who will produce the next generation and the ability of individuals to maintain their quality throughout many decades until death ensues.

The biological implications of reproduction are immense. The production of each new offspring provides an opportunity for another selection of genetic factors, and the growth and development of each young child infuses vitality into the species. These biological mechanisms enhance both the survival and the quality of survival of the species, and it is possible that they will be affected by the fact that man is now able to alter his pattern of reproduction.

Family size used to be limited to some extent by the crude and cruel effects of death and disease, but now it is restricted more effectively by artificial means. Such restriction seems to be necessary as a result of man's ingenuity and success in overcoming disease, creating a high expectation of long survival. Only in this way does it seem to be possible to avoid a population explosion and resultant famine, and to permit intensive and prolonged attention to be given to child rearing.

Nowadays, because of family limitation, the period devoted to child bearing is shorter than in the past, and, because of the concentration upon achievement of high quality of survival, a longer period is devoted to child rearing (*Figure 2.3*). This is illustrated by the pattern of family life experienced by young mothers in the two periods. The main period of child bearing at the present time lasts approximately 6½ years as compared with 18½ years in Milroy's day, and approximately 16 years are devoted to child rearing nowadays as compared with 8 years in the past. These changes permit wider flexibility in the time of child bearing and encourage preoccupation with child rearing practices; these features are reflected in the pattern of our social and cultural life.

Probably more important, however, than the altered pattern of life, is the fact that the reduction of family size to a uniformly small figure decreases the total opportunities for genetic selection. One hundred years ago young mothers had an average of 7 children, of whom 5 survived, whereas nowadays they have just over 2 children and almost all survive (*Figure 2.4*). It is difficult to predict the long-term effects of this phenomenon, but anxieties are being raised already (Cruz-Coke, 1968) and a thoughtful essay by the geneticist Theodosius Dobzhansky (1966) should be considered in this connection. He argued that human genetic diversity is not a regrettable caprice of nature, but is necessary to meet the changing demands of the environment. Such diversity is essential for biological adjustments to occur and in order that cultural advances and social

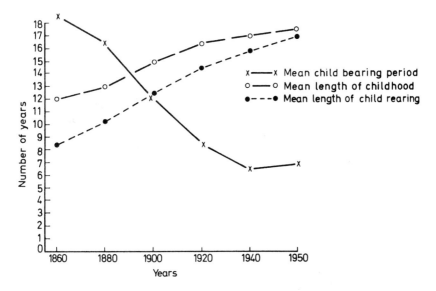

Figure 2.3. Child health from 1860 to 1950; family pattern of mothers 20–24 years of age at marriage (data from Registrar General, 1965)

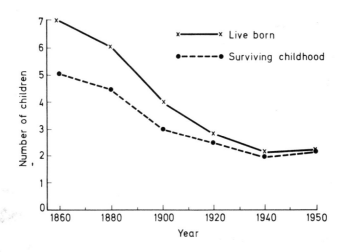

Figure 2.4. Child health from 1860 to 1950; family size of mothers 20–24 years of age at marriage (data from Registrar General, 1965)

13

equality may be possible. This thesis shows the importance of sufficient genetic diversity for human evolution, and demonstrates that biological planning requires consideration of the whole group and not of separate individuals. Only the future will reveal how successful we are in understanding and meeting these requirements; meanwhile we might speculate about our next steps.

Man's successful efforts in creating an excellent expectancy of survival were the result of the strong instinctive drives towards self-preservation which are shown by all living beings. Is it likely that he will cease to respond to these forces? Should we not accept that man will probably continue to seek to improve his lot, and that in doing so he might consider, in a decade or two, control of breeding? For example, infant survival prospects would be increased 10 per cent if child bearing were restricted to women aged 20–35 years. Whilst most will feel that the cost of such measures in terms of infringement of individual liberties is intolerable, and will argue in favour of making the prospects of those outside this age group the same as for those within it, they may not appreciate the extent to which our breeding habits are already influenced by educational, cultural and social factors. Although it is not easy to analyse the effects of these influences, their study is important for our consideration of the quality of survival, and perhaps this study will be included in medical school curricula or the future.

EMBRYOPATHY

The distinctive pattern of human reproduction relies upon the successful fertilization of a single ovum and its subsequent development to an embryo, followed by implantation of the placenta and nourishment of the fetus until it is ready to be born to the external world. This chain of events contributes to the quality of survival.

It is virtually impossible to know how many conceptions occur, but it is accepted that a considerable number, probably at least 20 per cent of all fertilized ova, are shed in the early weeks before implantation is complete. Most of these are blighted ova. A study of 237 cases of early spontaneous abortion showed a high incidence of abnormal embryos (Abaci and Aterman, 1968). The amniotic sac was intact in 91 cases, but only 16 of these embryos were normal. Other authors have reported similar findings (for example, Stevenson, 1967; Nayak, 1968). The number of defective fetuses which might result, if more of these defective embryos survived and continued intrauterine life, is considerable, but the fact that the successful continuation of the pregnancy depends to a major extent upon the state and function of the embryo must be regarded as a superb natural mechanism to prevent survival in such abnormal cases.

Attempts to salvage these early miscarriages seem inappropriate, and are seldom successful. What is important, and is being pursued to an ever-increasing extent, is to determine the causes of embryopathy and to find ways to avoid or correct the defects (Park, 1965). It is also important to find out how implantation of the healthy embryos can be made as favourable and successful as possible (Brown, 1948).

Once successful implantation has occurred, the prospects for the continued growth and development of the fetus are good. In fact, considering the extensive and complex changes which occur during this period, I never cease to marvel that disturbances occur so relatively infrequently. Nevertheless, despite the satisfactory outcome of most pregnancies, and the marked over-all improvement in results in recent years, deaths and defects continue to occur which might be prevented (Barron, 1968). The evidence for this statement is derived from comparisons of the vital statistics in different countries, and in different social groups within the United Kingdom.

VITAL STATISTICS

The perinatal and infant mortality rates of different countries vary considerably, with the affluent societies being grouped together with the lowest rates of all. The United Kingdom occupies the tenth position in the international list of infant mortality for 1969 (Wegman, 1972). Movement to the first position would be associated with considerably increased infant survival.

The Scandinavian figures are commendable. An interesting hypothesis has been put forward to explain these good results. For some years now therapeutic abortions have been performed on a large scale in Scandinavia, and are carried out at the rate of approximately 85 per 1,000 live births. This must remove some abnormal fetuses which would otherwise have survived and been included amongst the early deaths or defective children. It will be interesting to note in the coming years whether the freer availability of therapeutic abortion in the United Kingdom, which has been estimated to be already reaching a level of approximately 35 per 1,000 live births (Lewis, 1969), results in a reduction of the perinatal mortality rates.

Comparison of the vital statistics of the different social groups reveals the most striking and disturbing feature of these studies, namely that the relative differences in prospects for the fetus between the social groups are persisting despite marked over-all improvements in prospects for all groups. This is clearly shown in the studies of Baird (1945) and in the national perinatal mortality survey (Butler and Bonham, 1963). One measure of the significance of this is obtained by calculating the hypothetical results of obtaining social class 1 prospects for all social classes. This would result in a reduction of perinatal mortality by 22 per cent, with corresponding marked reductions in premature births, stillbirths and defects.

Many factors, obviously, contribute to these persisting differences between the social classes, some of which are known, others being the subject of speculation and many others awaiting discovery (McKeown, 1967). Women in social

15

class 1 are likely to be more favourably endowed genetically and intellectually as well as socially than women in social class 5, and also to have a better health record on the whole.

Early marriage is much more common in social class 5 than class 1. Information is available about the state of affairs in the year 1960/61, when the proportion of women marrying under the age of 20 years was 40.7 per cent in social class 5 and 9.9 per cent in social class 1 (Registrar General, 1965). Thus the majority of women marrying early come from the lower social classes and are the least prepared for the situation. Their lower educational attainments may leave them with little understanding of the problems they meet, they have the fewest and least suitable facilities and often find it difficult to seek help, advice and care. This may seem to be an extreme statement in the light of all the provisions that are made, and our long-standing tradition of health and welfare. It must be acknowledged, however, that the provision of services is not the same as their full and satisfactory utilization. The doctor/patient ratio is least favourable in the poorer areas, and patients find it difficult to seek out and obtain the help they require. Although they need help more than others, they seek it later. This is shown by comparing the time of first attendance for antenatal care of primiparae in the different social groups. In a city with two principal maternity hospitals, one serves the working class area and there two-thirds of the primiparae presented first in the third trimester. The other hospital serves a better class residential area and there two-thirds of the primiparae presented in the first trimester (Holt, 1965, unpublished data). In another study, Vaughan (1968) showed the close relationship between social factors and perinatal mortality. He compared mothers who had lost a baby in the perinatal period with others who had not suffered in this way, and he found that adverse social factors contributed to the loss of the baby in some cases as there was a significant correlation between: poor attitude towards, and late attendance for, antenatal care; poor diet; and serious family problems — and the loss of the baby. Therefore, social factors must be remembered in any consideration of survival.

One way in which social factors may affect survival is by influencing the quality as well as the availability of prenatal care. The national perinatal mortality survey (Butler and Bonham, 1963) of relatively few years ago showed that there were serious gaps in antenatal care and that these deficiencies occurred most frequently in the lower social classes. It is pertinent to recall some of the findings. There was no record of haemoglobin estimation in 33 per cent, of blood pressure in 16 per cent, and of Rhesus blood group determination in 5.5 per cent of the mothers. Furthermore, it was shown that in a small group which did not receive any antenatal care at all, the perinatal mortality rate was increased by 500 per cent. This report focused upon the need to ensure that antenatal services were provided and utilized as fully and efficiently as possible, and it has influenced the pattern of obstetric care in the United Kingdom in subsequent years. It is interesting to note that in the U.S.A., where they are so deeply concerned about their prevailing poor survival rates, they place prime importance upon the need to carry the medical and ancillary services to the groups who most need them (Stewart, 1967).

ANTENATAL PHYSIOLOGY

Although the achievement of better survival requires wider and more thorough application of efficient resources, these resources will not suffice alone, but need to be accompanied by an intensive study of human reproductive physiology. Activity in this field has increased dramatically in recent years, but much is still unexplored and our continued ignorance of this subject does not reflect to our credit. Half a century ago the wife of an American hog (pig) breeder, appalled at finding that less was known about the early growth and development of humans than of pigs, was instrumental in establishing the now famous Iowa Child Development Research Center. But even today we are being reminded that our knowledge of human developmental physiology is not as good as that of chickens and hens! After successfully feeding a completely artificial diet to a woman during the second half of her pregnancy, Allan and Brown (1968) nevertheless felt constrained to write as follows (reproduced by courtesy of the authors and publishers).

'It is a remarkable fact that knowledge of animal nutrition seems to be far in advance of that in human nutrition. For example, more is known of the amino acid and mineral requirements of the battery hen and the buxted chicken than is known of the human female and human infant. Disorders arising from trace element deficiencies are well documented in the animal and are important, but this field is virtually unexplored in man.'

Fortunately, the situation is not quite as depressing as it may appear, and much research is being done in this subject (for example, Dawes, 1968). The quest for a higher quality of survival has undoubtedly played some part in stimulating these intensive studies, but it was the appreciation of the vulnerability of this period which really prompted people to look more closely. Although it had been shown some years earlier that external influences could affect the outcome of pregnancy, these observations were concerned with severe and grossly adverse circumstances which we felt, somewhat complacently, seldom applied to the conditions within our civilization. For example, clinical and experimental studies showed that where there was a severely inadequate diet, the harmful results included increased rates of abortion, stillbirth, premature birth, mortality, and, experimentally at least, of malformations (Millen, 1962). Typical of these studies was that reported by Ebbs *et al.* (1942) (Table 2.1). He compared two groups of mothers, one of whom received a very inadequate diet, and he found a higher incidence of antenatal, natal and postnatal complications in this group, as compared with the other one. It can be calculated from Ebbs' results

17

that the provision of a fully satisfactory diet to the mothers in the experimental group would have resulted in the birth of 12 more babies and 5 less premature babies, the survival of 3 more infants in the first 6 months of life and a

TABLE 2.1
Effects of Maternal Nutrition on Infant

| Feature | Percentage showing unsatisfactory response | |
	Poor diet (120 cases)	Fortified diet (90 cases)
Antenatal condition	36.0	9.0
Miscarriage	5.8	0
Stillbirth	3.3	0
Prematurity	7.5	2.2
Condition in labour	24.0	3.0
Neonatal death	2.5	0
Maternal postnatal state	11.5	3.5
Infant postnatal state	14.0	0
Infant death	3.0	0

Data from Ebbs *et al.* (1942)

considerable reduction of morbidity for every 100 mothers concerned. However, this and similar studies were concerned with gross disturbances which were felt to occur only exceptionally, but evidence was accumulating to make us appreciate the general vulnerability of the intrauterine period. The devastating effects of maternal rubella early in pregnancy (Gregg, 1941) made us consider the possible hazards of other infections; and speculations about the dangers of drugs were intensified by the thalidomide disaster (Lenz, 1962). The demonstration of the effects of cigarette smoking (Simpson, 1957), the recognition of the phenomenon of intrauterine growth retardation (Gruenwald, 1964) and the realization that metabolic disturbances of the mother (such as phenylketonuria) might even poison the fetus (Allan and Brown, 1968) all helped to increase our concern for what was happening to the fetus *in utero*.

It is not just that a casual relationship has been shown between certain factors and the outcome of pregnancy, but that they have produced a definite reorientation of our thinking. For example, the importance of the fact that heavy smoking by a mother during pregnancy can result in her baby being 250 g or so lighter in weight at birth than would otherwise have been the case, lies not so much with the direct relationship between smoking and birth weight but rather with the speculation it creates, that if such a simple thing as smoking can do this, what other things might also affect the fetus.

These speculations are occurring very appositely at a time when we are realizing that the most important principle concerning a growing organism is its rate of change, and this principle applies to the fetal period just as much as to any other period of growth. Studying the rate of intrauterine growth by linking birth weight with the duration of gestation has led to an awareness of the syndromes of intrauterine growth retardation and malnutrition. This seems such a simple thing, yet its application to the study of small babies accounts for many recent advances in this field. Gruenwald (1964, 1967, 1968) calculated that at least one-third, and probably considerably more, of babies who are underweight in relation to their period of gestation, the so-called small-for-dates babies, had suffered intrauterine growth retardation of some kind, especially during the last trimester of pregnancy.

Not surprisingly, this is leading to a new, fuller look at maternal nutrition during pregnancy, and to questioning of some of the dietary restrictions which currently are imposed on pregnant women. The need for this is now further reinforced by the recent description of severe mental retardation in children resulting from exposure to high maternal serum levels of phenylalanine and allied substances during pregnancy (Allan and Brown, 1968). These mothers, but not their offspring, suffer from the inborn neurometabolic disorder of phenylketonuria. An analysis of 19 children of such mothers by Allan and Brown (1968) showed that 15 exposed *in utero* to phenylalanine levels of over 21 mg/100 ml were all retarded, whereas 4 children born to phenylketonuric mothers whose serum phenylalanine levels were less than 21 mg/100 ml were of average intelligence. Could similar disturbances occur with other disorders? It is clear that our search for high quality of survival requires continued study of the diet during pregnancy.

FETAL ENHANCEMENT

Whilst, on the one hand, attention is being given to the elucidation of the causes of death and abnormality which will lead to an improvement in the vital statistics, on the other hand, the question is being raised as to whether it is possible to promote the health of the fetus and to produce healthier and more intelligent babies. This idea does not seem quite so unreasonable as might have been thought just a few years ago, and has the feasible basis that every growing organism is susceptible to stimulation of its growth. This possibility accounted for the great interest aroused by Heyns' (1959, 1963, 1965) suggestion of a device for abdominal decompression to potentiate oxygen utilization by the fetus. This idea was developed after long study and was based upon the hypothesis that with decompression the uterus takes up a more 'physiological' spherical shape which enhances its contractions and the placental blood flow. This is thought to increase fetal oxygenation, and to reduce the discomforts of labour. So the infant is given a better start in life with less discomfort for the mother. The claims for this technique have not been supported by subsequent critical studies. Thus there are reports which state that there is no evidence of increased fetal oxygenation as estimated on fetal scalp blood (Mathews and Loeffler, 1968); no increase in intelligence of babies up to the age of 4 years as measured by the Merrill—Palmer test (Liddicoat, 1968); nor is labour easier (Castellanos, Aguero and DeSoto, 1968). This is just the beginning, however, and although this technique is not proving successful on a short-term follow-up, in our concern for survival for life we must realize that life lasts several decades and the long-term results of techniques such as this may prove to be more successful. There will undoubtedly be other attempts to promote the quality of survival at this early stage because our current attitudes direct us along this route.

As we try to promote fetal health, we need to be able to monitor our results — to know the status of the fetus at various times — and various techniques have been developed for this purpose. These include estimation of hormone levels during pregnancy (for example, Nachtigall *et al.,* 1968; Klopper, 1968), recording the fetal heart rate, chemical analysis of fetal blood, and amnioscopy and examination of amniotic fluid (for example, Wood, Lumley and Renou, 1967; Sharp, 1968). These investigations provide useful information about the maturity of the fetus and the presence of abnormalities, including growth retardation, especially in the later months of pregnancy, but they are still in an early stage of development and give evidence only of the grosser disturbances. Beard (1968) critically reviewed the role of these investigations and concluded that, whilst they are of value in certain situations, they must be associated with experienced clinical judgement. Furthermore, future developments should not be restricted to devising more and better tests only, but should explore on a broader basis the mechanisms of fetal loss in the poor socio-economic groups.

DIRECTION OF EFFORTS

In our search for quality of survival our efforts are directed in the following ways.

(1)   Seeking the causes of embryopathy.
(2)   Studying the intricacies of intrauterine physiology.
(3)   Applying resources to where they are needed most.
(4)   Attempting to potentiate the growth and development of each individual fetus

In this work the occasional voice is raised from time to time to ask if we are in danger of beginning to salvage the less fit individuals, but I see little evidence of this in connection with the efforts I have been describing, in contrast to the situation encountered after birth which I describe later. This opinion is based upon several factors. Firstly, the natural mechanisms for the rejection of abnormal embryos appear to be very effective. Secondly, although the perinatal mortality rate has been halved in the last 30 years (from 60 to 30), it has not been associated with any noticeable increase in abnormalities of the infants. Thirdly, the persisting strong influence of social conditions indicates the probability that we are dealing with basic disadvantages for development rather than defective fetuses. Fourthly, where attempts have been made to save fetuses that would otherwise be lost (for example, in cases of habitual abortion), the offspring from these saved pregnancies have proved to be normal and healthy (Shirodkar, 1967).

There would seem, therefore, much to be gained by continued efforts to promote survival of the fetus during pregnancy. This involves many types of research in different areas. Much of it will be concerned with intracellular function and molecular processes, whereas other activities will require operational research and the development of experimental services. These widely differing activities are devoted to the same end, namely the promotion of the quality of survival, and it is important that advances occur in all these aspects. In this respect, as in other spheres of child health described later, the research front is a broad one ranging from the study of minute detail to the clinical applications, and our task is to keep these extremes linked together.

It is clear that all of us who are interested in the quality of survival must be well informed about the events before birth. Because the paediatrician's ultimate aim and *raison d'être* is the promotion of the health of the next child-bearing generation, he must be interested in all antenatal events. He should not and cannot wait until birth, which, for the purposes of this discussion, may be considered the moment of survival to life.

Survival for Life: Birth Onwards

Independent life for each individual begins at the time of birth, which is also the end of the parasitic intrauterine phase. Although infants face many hazards at birth, relatively few casualties occur; the perinatal mortality rate for 1969 was only 23.0 per 1,000 total births (Registrar General, 1971), so that for the vast majority it is possible to speak of survival for life, rather than survival from death. This concept is important because it emphasizes the need to remember that life lasts several decades and throughout this time consideration must be given to the quality of survival during those decades and not just to survival alone.

The newborn infant starting his independent life is the end-product of the reproductive process. Because it is at this stage that paediatricians usually enter the picture, theirs is the task of accepting the end-products of reproduction as the new lives which will be in their care during growth and development. Some of the newborn are sick or defective and they require skilled and often intensive medical care if they are to survive at all. Neonatal and infant care has improved so much in recent years that many children alive today would otherwise have succumbed. However, sometimes the question is raised whether, through unnecessary and unselective efforts, we are salvaging more defective babies. This applies particularly to the smallest premature babies, the severely asphyxiated babies and those with gross congenital malformations.

THE SMALLEST SURVIVORS

The survival prospects of small premature infants are related to their birth weights — the smaller they are, the less their chance of survival. The quality of their survival is also related to their birth weight — the smaller the premature babies are, the less their chance of survival without some defect (Drillien, 1967; MacDonald, 1967). Although there is no absolute agreement about the precise extent of impairment, there is no doubt at all about the general pattern which results from prematurity. This is illustrated by Drillien's figures which she quoted just over a year ago in this lecture theatre (*Figure 2.5*). The proportion of

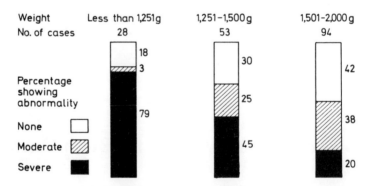

Figure 2.5. Survival of prematures: incidence of abnormalities according to birth weight (data from Drillien, 1967)

children with any abnormality, on long-term follow-up, in the three low birth weight groups (1,501–2,000 g, 1,251–1,500 g, and less than 1,251 g) was respectively 58, 70, and 81 per cent. The proportion of these defective children whose abnormalities were severe also increased with decrease in original birth weight. This was 1 out of 3 with a birth weight between 1,501 and 2,000 g, 2 out of 3 with a birth weight between 1,251 and 1,500 g, and practically all of them in the group with the lowest birth weight. These proportions are approximate.

The chance of these, the smallest surviving babies, escaping abnormalities is very small, and, as is shown, abnormalities are almost always severe. At birth there are few signs to indicate which of them will subsequently develop defects. In this respect they differ from the infants born with gross congenital malformations, which will be described later. Those babies who suffer complications during the neonatal period such as convulsions, cyanotic attacks and infections do less well than the others, but this tendency is by no means certain or absolute. Thus, medical care and attention must be given to each one alike. For the very small babies, however, the conclusion appears inescapable that at the present time this amounts to a salvage procedure, just as much as extensive surgery upon a malformed child.

Many of the smallest babies are stillborn, but if, as a result of our endeavours, an increased number survive, then, anticipating that they will face at least a similar incidence of abnormalities in later life as those currently surviving, there will be an increased number of children with severe defects (Table 2.2). This is illustrated by the following hypothetical calculation based upon the figures of

TABLE 2.2
Survival of Very Small Babies*

Fate of 30 babies under 1,500 g	Dead	Defective		Normal
		Severe	Mild	
Born at that weight	25	4	0	1
Born at that weight but 50% increased survival	15	11	0	4
Pregnancy continued with birth in next weight group 1,501–2,000 g	12	6	4	8

*Hypothetical analysis based on figures from the perinatal mortality survey (Butler and Bonham, 1963) and Drillien (1967)

the national perinatal mortality survey and Drillien's studies. Thus, if out of a group of 30 infants weighing 1,500 g or less the number surviving increased from 5 to 15, the number of surviving healthy children would be increased from 1 to 4, but the number of surviving babies with severe abnormalities would be increased from 4 to 11! The results have also been calculated on the basis of the whole group of 30 babies beign carried longer in pregnancy and being born in the next weight group (1,501–2,000 g) and experiencing the current prospects for any baby born in this group. In these circumstances the number of normal children would be increased to 8, whilst the number with severe abnormalities would only be increased to 6. This dramatically illustrates the truth of the old obstetric teaching that the best prospects for the infant are achieved by maintaining life *in utero*. The salvage procedure of intensive resuscitation of the very small infants increases survival, but only achieves this by increasing the proportion of those with severe abnormalities. Perpetuation of pregnancy is a much more physiological and satisfactory method of increasing survival without marked increase of abnormality.

It is much easier to argue from a hypothetical situation than to analyse what is happening in practice. Drillien (1967) attempted this and produced tentative evidence to suggest that techniques of neonatal care in recent years had resulted in an increased survival of defective infants. She studied the fate of infants weighing 1,500 g (3 lb) or less at birth in two five-year periods, 1948–1952 and 1955–1959 (Table 2.3). There were 12 more survivors during the later period than the earlier one, and this resulted in an increase of only 1 in the number of healthy children but of 11 in the number of moderately or severely handicapped, bearing out the figures of the hypothetical situation.

TABLE 2.3
Survival of Small Babies

Period	Survivors		
	Total	Normal	Abnormal
1948–52	18	12	6
1955–59	30	13	17

Data from Drillien (1967)

Before too despondent a view is taken of these figures, it must be remembered that the causes of this high incidence of subsequent occurrence of abnormalities in children of low birth weight are not known. If they are due to genetic or embryonic abnormalities, then a pessimistic view of our salvage efforts is justified; but if they are due to other causes, we should continue to try to overcome and to prevent them. There are two encouraging features in this connection. MacDonald (1967) noticed a lower incidence of neurological abnormalities in babies who had received intensive oxygen therapy. The numbers are small and not definitely conclusive, but they suggest the need to explore this point further. The second point is the fact that the incidence of subsequent abnormality is affected by social class (Drillien, 1967) (*Figure 2.6*). It is possible that the abnormalities in some of the small baby survivors are due to, or at least severely aggravated by, adverse social factors. This suggests that there is hope for amelioration and prevention.

Obviously with each small premature baby, paediatricians and obstetricians must ask why the birth occurred prematurely and why it could not have been prevented. Paediatricians will continue to care for and attempt to rear all such babies because those babies who will have subsequent abnormalities cannot be identified at this early stage. It is possible that in the future means will be found to prevent some of the abnormalities which now occur, but in the meantime our salvage operations in this field may be expected to yield a few more handicapped children than in the past.

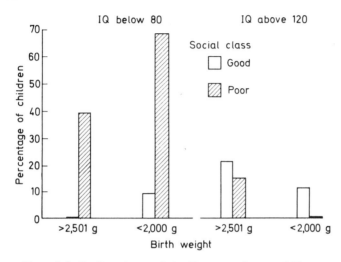

Figure 2.6. Quality of survival: intelligence at the age of 12 years, according to birth weight and social class (data from Drillien, 1967)

SEVERE ASPHYXIA

The problems facing the paediatrician with regard to the severely asphyxiated infant are similar to those presented by small premature babies. The more severe the degree of asphyxia and the longer its duration, the worse the outlook for the infant. However, it is not possible to be quite certain that a severely affected baby may not recover, and even be quite normal later on. Cases of extremely prolonged severe asphyxia with full recovery have been described (Holt, 1958a). Therefore the paediatrician cannot be selective but must resuscitate all or none, and obviously attempts resuscitation in all cases. Just as with the small baby, the paediatrician must seek out the causes of asphyxia and prevent it occurring, rather than being content just to salvage the severely asphyxiated babies.

25

In neither of these situations can I see that there is any indication for the practice of two levels of medicine — attempting full care in some cases and not in others. I strongly doubt whether such practice would even work. The intensity of effort and enthusiasm which strives constantly to improve medical care may occasionally lead to criticism of over-enthusiasm when a child survives with severe defects. However, against this must be balanced the benefits accruing in many other cases from this intensity of effort.

Somewhat different questions have to be faced in connection with babies born with obvious congenital malformations. The incidence of live-born babies with such malformations is 17.5 per 1,000 total births (Schutt, 1969), and approximately half of these are gross malformations. Babies with gross malformations often have multiple defects, not all of which are apparent at birth. Their prospects for survival are considerably reduced, and those who do survive are usually disabled to some extent so that their quality of survival is impaired. Knowing that there is a high risk of death and impaired quality of survival, doctors faced with a grossly abnormal baby at birth have to decide how far they should go in attempting to resuscitate the baby and to promote survival. Many doctors who face this dilemma have difficulty in discussing the subject, but such open discussion seems to be necessary. This can be done best by illustrating the problem with regard to the management of babies with spina bifida cystica.

SPINA BIFIDA CYSTICA*

The prospects for babies with spina bifida cystica who receive conservative treatment alone are poor. Frequently quoted figures are that 94 per cent die, 5 per cent survive with some disability, and 1 per cent survive and are normal. Laurence and Tew (1967) examined the survivors of 425 known cases of spina bifida in South Wales and found that there were 65 (15.3 per cent) living. Of these 65, 29 (6.8 per cent) had either no or only slight disabilities, and 36 (8.5 per cent) were severely disabled. Since the survivors who did well had only minor lesions without either hydrocephalus or limb paralysis from the beginning, these results paint an over-optimistic picture. Babies with extensive spina bifida with conservative treatment have slender prospects for survival and almost negligible hopes of being normal if they do survive.

The survival prospects of infants with spina bifida cystica increase dramatically with intensive and early surgical treatment. Early survival rates in the region of 80 per cent are now being reported (Eckstein and McNab, 1966; Lorber, 1968). Early treatment reduces the severity of lower limb paralysis (Sharrard et al., 1963) and controls the development of hydrocephalus (Lorber, 1968).

*Subsequent to the presentation of this section, Lorber (1971) reviewed his Sheffield experiences and revised his recommendations about treatment. This historic statement should be read in conjunction with this section.

The achievements of the medical and surgical treatment of spina bifida cystica are remarkable and will undoubtedly extend even further. If the best achievements currently reported were applied to the whole country, then in contrast to the past when there were, at most, 150 normal and 200 disabled survivors out of approximately 2,500 infants – this being the number of live-born babies with spina bifida expected annually (Smithells, 1965) – there would now be something like 500 normal and 1,500 disabled survivors. The actual state of affairs is somewhere between these extremes. Knox (1967) has reported that in Birmingham, where a varied and selective approach has been made to this subject, there was a survival rate of 21 per cent at 4 years of age, with just over half the survivors being disabled.

At the present time our intensive efforts do result in the survival of an increased total number of disabled children. A doctor faced with a baby with an extensive spina bifida lesion and some paralysis of the legs at birth knows now that, although intensive treatment will give much better results than conservative treatment, this requires the child to undergo many surgical procedures and prolonged medical care, and the prospect for survival as a normal child is still very small.

The cost of this increased survival of children with spina bifida is considerable. The cost to the child and his parents consists of a hospital-dominated early life with many operations and much emotional stress. The cost to the community is twofold, consisting of the increased total number of disabled children who need help and the actual expense of the concentration of medical manpower required for the necessary treatments. The situation here is similar to that concerning the very small baby, and it seems probable that the lessons learnt in both situations point to important principles; namely, that these salvage procedures succeed at the expense of increasing the number of handicapped individuals, and they are necessary only because of the failure of preventive medicine to determine and avoid the causes of the condition. This clearly indicates the need to focus our attention upon the preventative aspects in our research studies.

PARENTS' FEELINGS

Perhaps the most important question in all this discussion is the parents' own feelings about the subject. This topic has not been studied enough to date, but a brave report by Lawson (1968) from Australia should make us reflect upon it deeply. He interviewed the parents of 20 seriously malformed babies; 8 had severe spina bifida cystica, 9 were mongol children with associated heart or bowel defects, 2 had multiple defects and 1 had a severe cardiac defect. All the parents, except one mother, felt that it would have been better if the babies had not survived. Even in those cases where surgical procedures were attempted, the parents said they felt they had to go along with these attempts, but really deep

27

down hoped they would not be successful. Reading this report carefully, I feel that the parents expressed these opinions out of concern and love for their children. Perhaps they realized that if they found difficulty in accepting their child, how much more difficult it would be to expect others to do so?

MEDICAL PRINCIPLES

The doctor's dilemma in this situation has been discussed by others (Forrester, 1965b; Illingworth and Illingworth, 1965; MacKeith, 1967; Johnston, 1968; Sims, 1968; Zachary, 1968). I have studied these writings in reaching my own conclusions, which I shall outline in the hope that they will prove useful to others, although each individual must decide these questions for himself.

Treat the child, not the condition

Our first consideration must be for the child and his parents as individuals. Our prescription for treatment must be based upon what we consider best for them, and not simply the universal application of one policy to all.

Give equal consideration to all cases

I believe that it is impossible to practise two levels of medicine, striving fully in some cases and being casual in others. In this respect the striving and effort should be concentrated upon the decision making and should not be considered to be synonymous with action.

Recognize that extraordinary efforts are not always justified

The circumstances surrounding the birth of a severely malformed baby vary considerably. He may be the long-awaited baby of parents who can and wish to provide all the possible human and material help to promote survival; or he may be the unwanted offspring of a young unmarried girl who has no chance of being able to provide for him. If we accept that the presence of a severely abnormal fetus *in utero* justifies the termination of pregnancy in some cases, then I think we must accept that in some circumstances extraordinary attempts at salvage would be unwarranted. In this connection it must be remembered that the presence of a severely handicapped child in a family has the effect of reducing the number of subsequent pregnancies by approximately 25 per cent (Holt, 1958b). We must satisfy ourselves that we wish to expose the family to this inhibiting effect upon their family structure before pursuing extraordinary attempts to save the malformed baby.

28

Advise with the fullest knowledge

The parents are usually too dumbfounded to fully appreciate and discuss the situation, and I agree with Forrester (1965b) that it is wrong to place the whole burden of decision upon them. The doctor must actively advise, but to do so must seek as much background knowledge as possible. Nearly always the situation can be discussed with a close family representative. A general practitioner who knows the family well is better placed to advise in this situation than someone new to the case and possibly involved in the treatment. However, he must feel the strong backing of his consultant colleagues.

Respect inactivity by decision: condemn inactivity by default

This heading is self-explanatory.

Pursue treatment plans efficiently

Once a treatment plan has been recommended and agreed upon, it should be pursued as thoroughly as possible, whether this be an active or conservative approach.

These extensive problems which we face with regard to the survival and salvage of seriously malformed babies could easily absorb all our time and medical efforts, but they concern a relatively small number of babies; for the vast majority of our newborn their prospects at birth for subsequent survival are excellent. Malnutrition need not occur and most infectious diseases have been controlled. Their prospects for survival as healthy, active individuals are good, but quality of survival is not a static condition and we need to provide suitable circumstances for its stimulation and maintenance. It is questionable whether we always strive sufficiently to create the best conditions to maintain the quality of survival. The evidence is that we do not do so because we permit children to be exposed to stultifying adverse condtions.

SOCIAL LIMITATIONS

Attention has been drawn by several writers (Yudkin, 1967; Birch, 1968; Yudkin and Yudkin, 1968) to the fact that many of our children are expected to grow up in suboptimal surroundings. The physical environment is often unsatisfactory, especially for families with several children. Parents with their first child can normally find a home while their child is still young, although it may be often with their own parents (Young and Willmott, 1957). As families get larger, conditions become more difficult, and a recent government survey of families of two or more children showed a high incidence of overcrowding, affecting at least 11 per cent of the families, and lack of basic amenities, affecting at least 13 per cent of the families (Ministry of Social Security, 1967). This same report showed that 1 out of every 15 of the families in the survey did not possess sufficient resources to meet basic requirements. This alarming observation supports Abel-Smith and Townsend's (1966) finding that, in the United Kingdom, there are over half a million (5 per cent) children in families who subsist below the 'National Assistance' level, and 2.25 million children (17 per cent) in families whose resources are less than 40 per cent above the 'National Assistance' level (this level is considered to be an appropriate demarcation between subsistence and poverty). Not only are many children living in these poor conditions all the time, but many others can be brought into the same position, as very little additional stress is needed to aggravate the circumstances of vulnerable borderline families. For example, the Ministry of Social Security's survey of families with two or more children (1967) revealed that, where the father was in full-time employment, in only 2.4 per cent of them were their resources less than their requirements; but this figure rose to as much as 63.1 per cent in the families where the father was ill or unemployed. The presence of the father is important, at least as far as the physical amenities of the home are concerned, because in those cases where the fathers were sick, unemployed or absent, there was a much increased incidence of house deterioration and lack of amenities (Table 2.4).

Even more important than the physical facilities is the quality of care the children receive from their parents, especially their mothers. Bowlby (1952) and others (Ainsworth, 1962) have shown the importance of the early inter-personal environment for the development of children; but not all children receive such benefits. There are, for example, nearly 70,000 children in the care of local authorities in the United Kingdom. Some of them are in care for relatively short periods, but several thousands are in care for very long periods. In other cases the children may receive little support from their parents who may be too busy with their own activities to pay much attention to them, or may not want them or be interested in them. This rejection of children reaches considerable intensity at times and may even lead to physical abuse. It is extremely difficult to obtain evidence of ill treatment in such cases, but the appearance in hospitals of young children with bizarre injuries and fractures led to the recognition of the battered baby syndrome (Annotation, 1964). Since the recognition of this syndrome it is thought to account for many more deaths and serious injuries amongst young children each year than had been realized. The attitudes of parents who carry out these onslaughts is extremely complex and requires more intensive study. Some years ago Sheridan (1959) described a follow-up study of 100 mothers who had appeared before magistrates' courts for child neglect. Her report provided some insight into the depths of human wretchedness created by inefficiency, poverty and instability, but ended upon the cheerful note that a response is obtained sometimes to rehabilitation attempts when these are available.

It is difficult to describe and define all the requirements for good child rearing, but most of them fall into four main groups: the abilities of the parents

TABLE 2.4
Quality of Survival:
Social Factors and Family Amenities
(analysis of 280,000 families with 2 or more children)

Amenities	State of father		
	Full work	Sick/Unemployed	Absent
House defects:			
minor	11%	19%	17%
major	7%	20%	15%
Lack of amenities:			
minor	5%	2%	17%
major	8%	18%	10%
Overcrowding	11%	29%	31%

Data from Ministry of Social Security (1967)

to understand and fulfil the children's needs; the parents' personal attitudes towards their children; the amenities of the home; and the family's adjustment to the complexity of society which so often seems to add to parents' burdens and problems rather than acting for their benefit. In order to promote and to maintain a high quality of survival, favourable circumstances must be created, and these compose the cultural background in which the children are being brought up. Each group evolves for itself a cultural pattern which seems most appropriate and successful in the particular environment. It may be inappropriate and unsuccessful in a different setting, however, and it takes time for adjustment to occur. This sort of problem is being faced by an increasing number of children of new settlers in the United Kingdom who are being brought up according to the cultural patterns of their parents which were acquired in very different circumstances from those prevailing in their new country. Not surprisingly, these children experience difficulty in achieving their full potential. Study of these children reveals the extent of their difficulties and also illustrates the importance of cultural and environmental factors in child development and the maintenance of quality of survival. Pollak (1969) has completed an analysis of the development of all the 3-year-old children in a South London family practice (Table 2.5). All the children were born in the practice. Most of them could be divided into two

31

main groups: those born of indigent English parents and those born of recently settled English-speaking West Indian parents. There were, coincidentally, 75 children in each group, and there were no differences between the groups as regards antenatal and natal features. The two groups were practically identical

TABLE 2.5

Quality of Survival: Comparison of Development of 75 3-year-old West Indian Children Born in London with 75 3-year-old English Children in the Same Area

Developmental feature	Mean values for West Indian children expressed as percentage of mean values for English children
Motor	97%
Personal–social	78%
Adaptive	34%
Language	32%

Data from Pollak (1969)

with regard to the acquisition of motor skills, but the development of the children of the West Indian parents was delayed as regards personal-social skills, and was markedly inferior as regards adaptive and language behaviour. This shows that as a result of a different cultural pattern of child rearing, the children were less well equipped to deal with a competitive world and to take advantage of growing up in our particular environment. This is an example of the extensive effects which can result from cultural deprivation. Much attention has been focused on this in recent years (for example, Pringle, 1965; Douglas, 1966; Booth, Dardarian and Satherthwaite, 1967), and money and effort are being spent particularly on the educational side to remedy the harmful effects of cultural deprivation. These efforts are starting, however, relatively late in life. The effects of such deprivation upon child development are apparent to the perceptive eye of a developmental child health specialist in infancy, long before the child reaches school age. The words of one such specialist, Egan (1966), which have been already put before us by Yudkin (1967), deserve repetition. She wrote as follows (reproduced by courtesy of the author and publishers).

'I can readily pick out children whose development is retarded simply through lack of social experience and stimulation. Most of these children are well-nourished, and their motor development appears to be unaffected by long hours spent in a confined space. But their social behaviour and play during the first year often shows a characteristic withdrawal.'

Clearly it would be wrong of us as doctors to ignore the problems of cultural deprivation. If we are truly concerned about child health and anxious to promote the quality of survival, then we must collaborate with colleagues in the social and educational fields, because we are in an ideal position, as we examine young babies, to detect deprivation in the earliest stages and, by parental guidance in the child health clinics, to avert many of its consequences and complications. The value of this work is not immediately obvious nor readily demonstrable, but it is nevertheless considerable, and its potential contribution towards the mental health of both parents and children has yet to be fully appreciated. It is unfortunate that its more energetic pursuit is hindered in various ways. For example, our preoccupation with 'organicity' is leading us to focus upon the detection of abnormalities in the few, and to the possible neglect of the practice of preventive and anticipatory guidance for the vast majority. Furthermore, because the work does not concern acute and dramatic emergencies and lead to easily and immediately demonstrable results, it does not receive the support and attention of work which has this appeal. It is more interesting to treat a case of advanced rickets, but more valuable to prescribe cod liver oil in time. It is dramatic to reconstruct a dislocated hip, immobilizing the patient for a long period to do so, but this need not be necessary at all if a simple examination is made of the hips of each new baby. The practice of preventive medicine of this kind requires continuous application, without the stimulation of frequent medical conundrums or dramas, together with an ability to recognize potential abnormalities in their earliest stages.

RANGE OF NORMALITY

While we are considering the skills of doctors concerned with the promotion of child health and the quality of survival, it is pertinent to point out that the changes in the pattern of survival are making it necessary to alter our clinical methods. We now need to have a clearer idea of the nature of normality and its range and to be able to detect variations from normality.

When one considers the vast numbers of mature healthy babies that are born, it is easy to think of them all as being pretty much the same, but I have tried to make it clear that they differ considerably with regard to genetic endowment and intrauterine experiences. Individuals are not equal even at birth. This human diversity is essential to us as a group, so that our group has the flexibility to adjust to diverse situations. Consequently, it is neither possible nor desirable to define an optimum pattern for all human individuals. For example, many people admire plump round-faced babies and remark about their health, but obese babies often become obese adults and suffer the consequences of hypertension, coronary artery disease and early death (Lloyd, Wolff and Whelan, 1961). Thus it would seem that obesity is not an asset for the survival of children growing up in our over-fed affluent societies. However, it is possible that the

33

obese state may be more advantageous in other environments; for instance, who knows when the ice age will return?

Marked discrepancy between an individual's characteristics and his environment may lead to considerable conflict and may not be to the advantage of the individual. For example, a high level of intelligence would normally be considered to be an asset, but if the individual's abilities are very different from those of his parents and friends he may suffer acute distress and frustration. An asset that many would prize is here turned to a disadvantage for the individual. Thus it is important to see individual qualities in the light of the environmental circumstances, and it is difficult to define an optimum or ideal status for individuals which would apply all the time and in all conditions.

Despite these facts — the difficulty of defining the optimum state for the individual and the need to relate individual characteristics to the environment — there is now a strong trend towards a demand for development in one particular direction; namely, towards high quality, especially with regard to intellectual skills and attainments. This has made us look again at those children who show inferior performance and to speculate whether some 'inferior' children have suffered some form of damage which might have been prevented, and are not just children at the lower end of the range of normal distribution.

The possibility of the existence of another state of affairs was really brought home to us by Lilienfeld and Pasamanick (1954), who performed an epidemiological analysis of the outcome of pregnancies and demonstrated the existence of what they called a continuum of damage. The hypothesis was that damage, especially cerebral damage, might occur to varying degrees, resulting in the production of some very severely damaged babies, others less severely affected, some mildly affected and others escaping damage altogether. This hypothesis of a spectrum or continuum of damage was invoked to account for such problems as clumsiness, epilepsy and behaviour disorders experienced by some children. This idea received support from the interesting researches of Prechtl and his colleagues (Prechtl, 1967). He studied the relationship between antenatal and natal events and the subsequent state of the children. Because he did not study babies with gross abnormalities, his observations are of particular interest for the light they shed on this interface between the normal and abnormal. He demonstrated a cumulative effect of adverse pregnancy factors which contribute to the occurrence of impaired performance and neurological difficulties as the children grow older.

The concept of a continuum of damage is not accepted universally, and it is probable that the situation is not as simple as originally stated, but these and similar studies pointed the way to our realization of the possibility of there being preventable causes to account for the problems of some children with inferior abilities. In this context the syndromes of the clumsy child and minimal cerebral palsy were defined and described (Bax and MacKeith, 1963). Thus we now accept that children who are not doing well at school, are clumsy, show behaviour problems and so forth may have an organic basis for their difficulties. They represent the milder end of the impairment of full quality survival. These children must be detected and diagnosed, and if their difficulties can be prevented or they can be treated successfully, then it will help to improve the quality of survival of the group as a whole.

TESTS AND MEASUREMENTS*

This attention to the performance of children has started a major reorientation in our approach to children's disorders. It is necessary to examine them to determine whether they show inferior performance in any way, and then to decide whether or not this represents some form of minimal damage. We are in fact looking carefully at the quality of surviving children. But how do we assess quality? Precise and accurate techniques are evolving for the examination of children which have some of the features of a refined clinical neurological examination combined with some features of a psychological test procedure. This work is being done in schools and special research projects such as the Isle of Wight epidemiological study of childhood defects (Rutter, Tizard and Whitmore, 1969). It is seldom being done in hospitals because the children are not ill in the normal sense of the word and so resent referral to a hospital. In developing this work it is necessary to consider the basis of the various tests and measurements which we perform.

Most clinical medical work is based upon the detection of abnormal signs. In many instances we try to elicit a sign which is present only in abnormal situations, and absent in normal situations. For example, a heart murmur. The more complete this separation, the more satisfactory is the clinical sign. Another type of clinical sign is that where the nature of the response elicited is different in abnormal states from normal states, as in the case of the Babinski response. A further example of this type of sign is the patellar tendon reflex, where gross deviation from normal is detected readily; however, here minor degrees of variation are less easy to judge and require considerable 'clinical judgement'.

In paediatrics, the detection of abnormal signs is both helped and hindered by the fact that age affects the appearance and disappearance of the various responses which can be used as clinical signs; and this has to be taken into account. The rate at which these responses evolve with age determines the way in which they are used for clinical measurements. This is illustrated in *Figure 2.7a.* If the period AB between the first appearance of the response at A in any child and the presence of the response in all children at B is small, then that

*This section is abstracted from a lecture given by the author whilst Mayne Visiting Professor of Child Health, University of Queensland, Australia, in 1967.

particular response can be used as a satisfactory clinical sign — the presence of the response before age A and absence after age B indicates abnormality. For example, the Moro and the asymmetrical tonic neck responses are present in early infancy but cannot normally be elicited after the age of 6 months and 7 months respectively. The presence of these responses after these ages indicates immaturity or abnormality of the nervous system. Another skill which develops

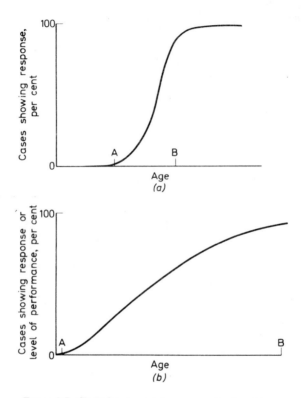

Figure 2.7. Clinical tests and measurements related to age

rapidly is the acquisition of language, which has been defined as the symbolization of thought, and can be shown in tests of the child's ability to recognize the nature of objects and the significance of their relationship to each other (Reynell, 1969). This skill develops most rapidly between the ages of 1½ and 2½ years and is normally complete by 4½ years. Failure to acquire symbolic language at this early age is a clear sign of language disorder. Still another age-dependent sign is derived from the Fog test, which is particularly useful in detecting motor immaturity (*Figure 2.8*). The child is asked to stand on the sides of his feet and the observer notes any movement of the arms and hands. The majority of normal children under the age of 10 years show marked supination of the fore-arms, but it is seldom seen after this age. There is a fairly sharp change in this sign after the age of 10 years, so that the detection of a positive response to this test in older children is a sign of motor immaturity. These few examples show the importance of studying the nature of children's responses at different ages, and where a rapid change in the response occurs over a short age span, it is possible to use this information for the construction of reliable clinical signs.

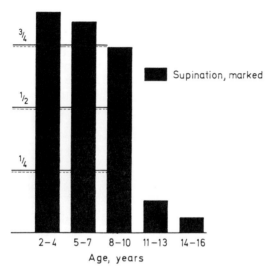

Figure 2.8. Fog feet–hands test results with normal
children (data from Fog and Fog, 1963)

In contrast, many children's skills do not show such a sharp transition with age, and the level of performance increases only gradually over a wide age span, as shown diagrammatically in *Figure 2.7b*. If we are concerned with a skill of this type and wish to use it as a clinical measurement, then we have to take account of the following points.

(1) The measurements must be standardized on the normal population, and age variations and standard deviations have to be calculated.

(2) The procedure for carrying out the measurement must be described precisely and later followed accurately in order to obtain reliable and repeatable results.

Then, the most suitable measurements for use in the assessment of functional skills are those with a small deviation and a large age increment. These criteria make it much easier to detect those results which fall outside the range of normal variation. It is also important to check the reliability of the measurements when carried out at different times by the same observer, and by different observers.

Performing careful clinical measurements of this nature is different from much of the traditional type of clinical practice, and many doctors do not find it easy to obey the discipline required to carry out these scientific measurements. This discipline, in fact, is precisely what we are now developing in child health practice in order to detect accurately and to define those children who are showing inferior performance. However, the detection of minimal cerebral disorders is not made easier by the debatable value of some of the tests in present use. For instance, the Purdue pegboard test of manipulative function (Table 2.6) has such a small age increment that the variation of the test score by only one or two points may be wrongly interpreted as indicating motor immaturity. Berges and Lezine (1965) described a series of arm and hand gestures which children are asked to imitate. The performance to be expected at different

TABLE 2.6
Minimal Normal Scores from Purdue Pegboard Test

Age	Using dominant hand	Using non-dominant hand	Using both hands
6–7 years	9	8	8
8–9 years	11	9	9
10+ years	13	11	10

Data from Rapin, Tourk and Costa (1966).

ages has been described, but it is difficult to interpret the significance of the results because of the many different skills required in the performance of these tests, which include visual acuity, general intelligence, motor power, co-ordination, perception of gesture, and of sequence, and co-operation.

In this type of clinical work, therefore, it is important to obtain meaningful and reliable results in order to be able to detect minor abnormalities from poor but otherwise normal performance, and also to reduce as much as possible the number of factors which may influence the result. I tried to achieve this in a simple test of manipulative function which I devised a few years ago (Holt, 1965). The child is asked to place small pegs one at a time from a box into a cup and the number in a set time is recorded. This task only requires the ability to pick up the peg, move the hand into position and drop the peg into the cup. Although these simple skills can be performed by quite young children, the speed of performance increases in an almost linear fashion to a peak between 8 and 10 years of age. The child is also asked to place the pegs into a pegboard as quickly as he can. This requires the slightly more complicated manipulative manoeuvre of turning the peg and inserting it into the hole. The speed of performance of this task also increases in an almost linear fashion with age. The actual number of pegs placed on the board also depends upon the child's age and is related to his score in the first test (*Figure 2.9*). Consequently,

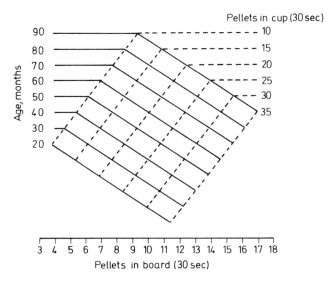

Figure 2.9. Pellets in the cup/in the board related to age (reproduced from Holt, 1965, by courtesy of the publishers)

the expected pegboard score can be predicted in advance and then compared with the actual score obtained. A score lower than expected indicates the presence of manipulative impairment. This simple technique eliminates many variables, and permits an assessment of manipulative skill to be made without the necessity of making allowances for such factors as the child's level of intelligence.

Thus, in the practice of child health, as we are increasingly called upon to detect those children with inferior performance and minor disorders, we must develop new clinical techniques which demand a high precision of scientific measurement. Such methods will be increasingly important in the future as we reach towards a high quality of survival, and attempts have begun to incorporate them into the examination of school children.

COMMUNITY CHILD HEALTH SPECIALISTS

I hope it is clear from what I have said that I believe that the present-day practice of child health requires a thorough understanding of normal child development and its variations as expressed in the environment of the family, school and community. It is no longer adequate to base teaching about child health upon the Oslerian tradition at the bedside of the sick person (Holt, 1966a; Forfar, 1968); but it seems that it is not considered that those working in child health services outside hospitals require the intensity of postgraduate training that is available to others. Perhaps the most marked example of this discrepancy is the fact that medical officers who advise about the needs of children experiencing school difficulties and possibly in need of special education, many of whom have complicated medical and intellectual difficulties as well as secondary emotional disturbances, are required to receive only three or four weeks' special postgraduate training for the purpose. They are then equipped to make recommendations which may have a major long-term influence upon the child's life. In contrast, a consultant radiologist will receive about ten years' postgraduate training to be able to report the result of a child's radiograph. Far better for your child to have pneumonia than impaired development! The situation is reminiscent of the topsyturvy state of affairs in Samuel Butler's Erehwon.

The promotion of child health in the United Kingdom depends largely upon the medical officer of the local authority health services (Table 2.7). Recent

TABLE 2.7
Attendance of Children at Different Types of Clinics

Type of clinic	Age of child	
	Under 2 years	2–4 years
General practitioner	4%	8%
General practitioner and local authority combined	9%	4%
Local authority	74%	31%
None	13%	57%

Data from Central Health Services Council (1967)

figures show that few general practitioners hold child health clinics. These figures also show the sharp decline of attendance at any clinics after the first two years, just at a time when the child is particularly vulnerable to adverse circumstances and when developmental defects might become evident. We cannot really claim to have a comprehensive and adequate child health service yet, but there are

40

indications that the need for child health specialists to be deployed on a broader front than in the past is now being recognized. For example, the Sheldon Report (Central Health Services Council, 1967) called attention to the need to promote the health and welfare of young children; the discussions at the 1968 conference of the Association for the Study of Medical Education on paediatrics education contained frequent references to the need for more child health specialists; and the Institute of Child Health in London has initiated the first three-term university postgraduate course on developmental paediatrics and child assessment.

To summarize this brief review of some of the present-day problems in child health, it is clear that we are concerned on the one hand with a relatively small number of seriously damaged children whose requirements for medical and surgical care are absorbing much of our best talents and money, and on the other hand with considerable numbers of children who are exposed to less than optimal circumstances which may affect their development. If we are to promote the quality of survival, we cannot afford to ignore this large group of disadvantaged children. In the years to come the practice of preventive child health should be stressed to an increasing extent, and new clinical techniques be evolved to assess the quality of performance. This has already been said by our president (of the Royal College of Physicians) in his lecture entitled 'Health of the World Tomorrow' (Rosenheim, 1968). Whilst acknowledging medical triumphs, he points out that salvage surgery reflects failure of prevention, and emphasizes the need for teamwork and the recognition of the individuality of the patient. The need for teamwork is particularly evident in the medical approach to those children who require assistance to appreciate the full quality of their survival (that is, the handicapped), and it is in this work that we see to the best many of the collaborative efforts which are necessary in the modern practice of child health.

Survival with Help: the Handicapped

Handicapped children are those who cannot achieve their full potential quality of survival without help in addition to what they would normally receive. The precise number of such children is not known, but it is generally accepted that 1 out of every 10 children has some handicap and that it exists to a disabling extent in half of them. Even higher figures than these have been recorded. Such high figures frequently cause surprise, but should not do so when it is recognized that the sum total accrues from three main sources: that is, from the salvage of the very young and malformed babies; by the survival of those who might have been expected to succumb in the past from infections; and, lastly, as a result of our checks upon performance which lead to the detection of children with definite but less severe defects.

It is important at this point to remember that these children are handicapped as a result of some occurrence early in life. Sometimes the defects are noticed at birth or shortly thereafter, but other problems are not recognized for some years despite the fact that the trouble may have been caused much earlier. Where the impairment is apparent early, the parents never know their child as 'normal', which greatly increases the emotional problems of both the child and his parents. Early impairment also limits the child's first learning opportunities. Both these factors cause the child to suffer from secondary complicating handicaps, particularly emotional disturbances and deprivation of learning experiences.

Handicapped children used to be accepted as they were with little question as to the causes of their condition. Deaf children were also dumb children until it was realized that the dumbness was due to the lack of appreciation of auditory stimuli in early life, and that by early training the dumbness could be reduced. Textbooks continue to carry pictures of so-called 'classical' cerebral palsy showing deformities and possibly dislocation of the hips, all of which can be prevented by early medical and surgical treatment. Fortunately, we are slowly moving from the state of mind which passively accepts handicapped children and pityingly offers charitable help, to that which recognizes that these children require the full range of medical help, and not charity alone, if they are to reach their full potential quality of survival. This requires that they be detected and diagnosed as early as possible, their problems studied scientifically and assessed according to their individual needs, and a programme of continuing care worked out to ensure continuity and integration of efforts.

EARLY DIAGNOSIS

In trying to make an early diagnosis of any defect, it helps to know which children have been exposed to those detrimental experiences which might lead to the development of particular defects. This is the basis of the 'at risk' concept (Sheridan, 1962) which led to the compilation of 'at risk registers' by many local authorities. If a particular baby experiences any one of a listed number of potentially harmful genetic, antenatal, natal and postnatal factors, then his name is placed on a register to ensure that he has repeated careful examinations until it is quite clear that he is not handicapped. The working of these registers has been described by several writers (such as Rogers, 1968; Thomas, 1968) but criticized by others (for example, Oppé, 1967; Richards and Roberts, 1967). These registers have not been as successful as many had hoped. The initial thinking that if only the correct criteria for detection could be defined, it should be possible to get most, if not all, of the handicapped children from the at risk group, ignores the evidence that some handicapped children have a completely negative past history. In addition, too many and poorly defined criteria resulted in the overloading of the registers and to their subsequent adverse criticism. The most important reason for the unsatisfactory state of many registers, I believe, is that they have been developed as administrative procedures rather than clinical aids (Holt, 1968). The basic at risk concept is a good one, and it is its application that has been unsatisfactory. Because we are so concerned with the quality of survival, this approach should not be abandoned, but attempts should be made to make it work effectively. It should be used in a clinical sense, with the administrative machinery facilitating the flow of vital information between the clinical units concerned in this work, as shown in *Figure 2.10*.

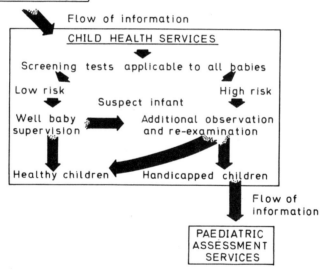

Figure 2.10. Organization of clinical services for the early detection of defects (reproduced from Holt, 1966, by courtesy of the Editor)

One of the most interesting results described by those with experience of at risk registers is that it focused their interest upon the young child and encouraged them to seek further training in developmental examinations. This resulted in the earlier detection of handicapped children in both the at risk and the non-risk groups (Rogers, 1967). Such clinical training and experience obviously promotes early detection and thus enhances the quality of survival

43

of the handicapped child. A problem facing us as medical teachers is that it is difficult to convey this training to those who are most likely to benefit from it because they are isolated in their work. A few years ago I studied the referral of children with cerebral palsy to an assessment and treatment unit situated in an area where there was a long-standing tradition of teaching about early developmental diagnosis (Holt, 1969, unpublished data). The results were disappointing. The proportion diagnosed in the first year of life was small, often being less than 10 per cent and only reaching 17.5 per cent in the best year of the study. Further investigation revealed that those who were aware of the teaching about and emphasis upon early diagnosis were finding the cases early, and the later diagnosed cases were coming from those doctors furthest from the teaching centre − in all senses.

Early referral of handicapped children is not easy. The difficulties of acquiring the clinical skill and experience to detect abnormalities in their earliest stages are considerable. In addition, a doctor suspecting possible abnormality in a young baby may be reluctant to refer the infant to a hospital clinic, especially if this involves a long journey, for fear of unnecessarily arousing the parents' anxieties. This is one of several reasons for the failure of early referral which emerged from this study (Table 2.8). If a child health specialist

TABLE 2.8
Failure of Early Referral in Cerebral Palsy

Diagnosis		
Not made	Suspected, without further action	Made, but no referral
Baby not examined	Difficulty of diagnosis	Doctor unaware of facilities
Doctor inexperienced	Failure to confirm	Doctor thinks early treatment is not important
Failure of follow-up	Fear of upsetting parents	

were able to examine the infant causing anxiety in the congenial and familiar surrounding of the child health clinic, many of these problems of early referral would be overcome.

The emphasis on early diagnosis of defects has led to the development of a whole new range of clinical techniques. The old-fashioned attitude of waiting until the child is able to co-operate in tests ignores the importance of the early years of learning and development and must be abandoned if we are to detect and treat cases as early as possible. The new techniques are based upon the philosophy that if the child cannot respond to a particular test, then that test must be revised into a form to which he can respond. Also, the examiner must learn how to interpret each individual response of these very young children. Typical examples include the free-field tests of response to auditory stimuli used to detect hearing defects in young babies, and the application of puppet audiometry which enables a good evaluation to be made of the hearing for pure tones as early as 18 months (Holt and Reynell, 1967). Visual function can also be tested quite early by using the techniques devised by Sheridan (1960). All these tests appear very simple and easy, but it requires considerable skill and experience of their use to get appropriate responses from young children and to make reliable observations. The tests are really an exploration of the physiological responses of young growing organisms to external stimuli, and yield a great deal of information about the child in addition to the test result. For example, the degree of alertness and ability to deal with conflicting stimuli, such as simultaneous visual and auditory stimuli, can be studied at the same time as testing the child's response to the individual stimuli. The apparently simple tests have been devised only after much scientific investigation. Sheridan, for example, in deciding which symbols she should use in tests of visual function, had first to find out the order in which young children learnt to recognize vertical, horizontal, oblique and curved lines – as scientific an exploration of neurophysiological perception as one could wish for!

SCIENTIFIC ANALYSIS

Diagnosis is not, in the case of handicapped children, the summit of the medical exercise, but is the first step towards a long and complex programme of continuing care. In order to work out this programme, each child's individual difficulties must be evaluated as fully and scientifically as possible. This need for a scientific approach will be illustrated by brief reference to three items: namely, the value of planned observation; the use of electromyography for the analysis of locomotor problems; and methods of analysis of language disorders.

Various observation techniques have been used in some of the more sophisticated research studies for many years (Wright, 1960). An example of a planned observation of a clinical problem is the timed observation study made of a small group of young hemiplegic children in a setting specifically arranged to encourage the use of both hands together. A note was made at regular intervals of the pattern of their hand use, and at the end of the period the frequency of use of both hands together was calculated as a percentage of the total number of opportunities. The range was from 5 to 61 per cent, showing, incidentally, the marked range of severity of involvement in infantile hemiplegia. Half the children were then given intensive treatment for 3 months, after which both groups were re-examined; 3 out of 4 in the treated group showed considerable improvement, but all 4 in the non-treated group had deteriorated. This study shows how one observation technique enabled us to make a quantitative assessment of the degree of impairment of hand function in these children and also of their response to treatment. Observation techniques are being used to an increasing extent in clinical assessment procedures for handicapped children and they could be usefully applied in other clinical fields.

Electromyography contributes to the understanding of locomotor problems (Holt, 1966b). The two children in *Figure 2.11* appear to have similar forms of

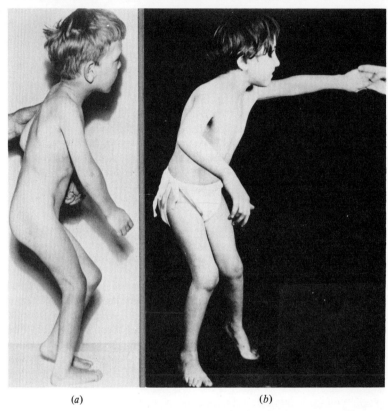

(a)   (b)

Figure 2.11. Two children (a, a boy; b, a girl) apparently with similar forms of cerebral palsy and associated deformities

cerebral palsy and associated deformities, but it is only when electromyography is carried out that it becomes clear that different groups of muscles are active in the two children (*Figure 2.12*). In the case of the boy (*Figure 2.12a*) the hamstring and gastrocnemius muscles are active, whereas the quadriceps and anterior tibial groups show little activity. The reverse situation is seen in the case of the girl in whom most activity is present in the quadriceps and anterior tibial muscles. The neuromuscular problems and the types of treatment required are quite different in these two children. This type of analysis, showing

46

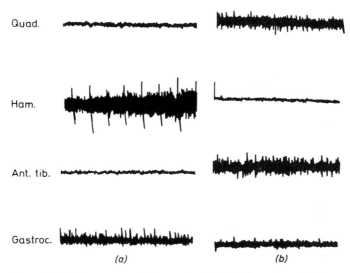

Quad.

Ham.

Ant. tib.

Gastroc.

(a)   (b)

Figure 2.12. Electromyographic records of the children shown in Figure 2.11a and b

which muscles are active and which quiescent, requires the use of surface electrodes only and so does not distress the children. This method also enables us to assess the results of treatment. *Figure 2.13* shows the electromyographic records of a child standing with flexed knees and maintaining his upright position by constant contraction of the quadriceps muscles. The application of a short leg brace stabilizes his position and allows the quadriceps to relax. The new position puts tension on the hamstrings which now show activity. *Figure 2.14* shows how the electromyographic records can be used to assess the results of drug treatment in children with cerebral palsy. This illustration is taken from a controlled clinical trial and shows that Valium effectively reduced excessive resting, and postural and reflexly stimulated muscle activity, to the benefit of the child (Holt, 1967).

The third example chosen to illustrate the application of scientific techniques to the study and assessment of the problems of handicapped children concerns the analysis of language disorders. The speech—language formula (*Figure 2.15*) illustrates the many steps involved in the complex language processes. Incoming auditory messages have to be heard, understood and remembered, and then linked with thought and language processes. Expression should involve a mobilization of thought processes, integration with speech patterns and then vocalization as intelligible speech. Continuous monitoring of speech takes place to provide the individual with control over his own utterances. Failure in monitoring

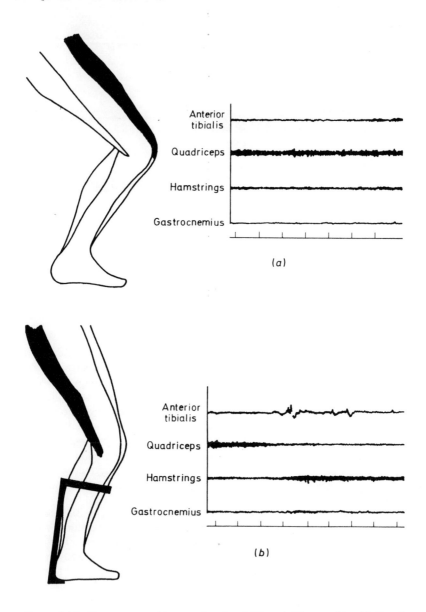

Figure 2.13. Electromyographic records of a child aged 12 years (a) *with flexed knees and* (b) *with short leg brace stabilizing the knee*

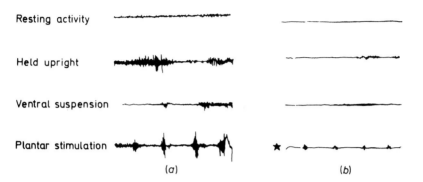

Resting activity

Held upright

Ventral suspension

Plantar stimulation

(a)   (b)

result obtained only with large dose of Valium

Figure 2.14. Electromyographic records of a child aged 2½ years (a) *without and* (b) *with Valium treatment. All records were taken from the anterior tibial muscle*

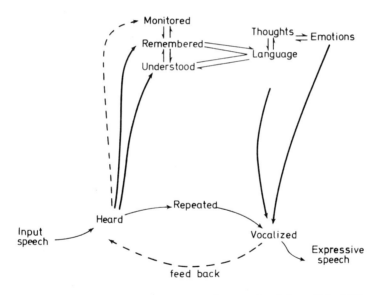

Figure 2.15. The speech–language formula (reproduced from Holt, 1966, by courtesy of the Editor)

confuses the individual and inhibits speech. Repetition and imitation of speech without higher cerebral analysis produces a meaningless parrot-like type of speech. In learning to analyse the language disorders of severely handicapped

49

children step by step, we have devised methods which are applicable to all speech-impaired children. *Figure 2.16* shows the site of neurological block in the case of a child with one type of expressive aphasia. He is unable to make use of his understanding of speech to formulate (encode) his thought processes into expressive speech. In consequence, his speech is disorganized and unintelligible,

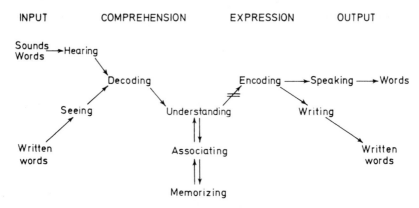

Figure 2.16. Analysis of a child with one type of expressive aphasia (reproduced from Holt, 1969, by courtesy of the Editor)

despite the fact that he has no articulatory disorder as shown by his ability to repeat sounds and words provided that cerebral analysis is not involved. By studying each step in the language process carefully, it is possible to define the point of disturbance, just as one might do in the analysis of a biochemical problem. By these illustrations I have tried to show that if a handicapped child is to realize his full potential, he must have a careful scientific analysis of his problems.

AND EVEN MORE

A scientific approach alone is not enough. The findings must be interpreted in terms of what they mean for each child and his particular pattern of development. Consider, for example, a child who is so physically handicapped that he cannot move about and is thus completely dependent on others. He can never learn to promote or inhibit personal relationships by going towards or away from someone, and sometimes learns to control personal relationships by behaving in a fractious way to gain attention, and even sometimes in a repulsive way when he wants people to leave him alone. The prescription of a wheel chair means more than just a method of conveyance; it gives a new meaning to life as he can now come and go as he pleases. But an old worn chair of unsuitable size does not make one feel that one is gaining the fullness of life!

The problems of the handicapped cannot be quickly overcome as one might overcome the problems of an acutely ill child. They can be ameliorated; learning deficiencies can be overcome and secondary complications prevented, as the children and their parents are guided towards their fullest possible life, thereby promoting their quality of survival. Inevitably this work involves many people — doctors, nurses, psychologists, therapists, teachers, and others, over a long period, not all of whom may be involved at any one time. The actions of each specialist so far as they affect the child and the management of his problems, are important to everyone else concerned either at that time or in the future. Consequently, success occurs only where there is integration of action and the following of an accepted plan of continuing care. The concept of continuing care is of paramount importance to the handicapped child.

As we search for a high quality of survival for all children, those whose survival needs assistance cannot be neglected. Sympathy and charity alone do not lead to either the understanding of the handicaps or the promotion of the quality of survival. A scientific study of their problems and evolution of a plan of continuing care will, however, lead to both greater understanding and the promotion of the quality of survival. Parents are going to demand this for their children, as was recognized in the Todd Report (Royal Commission on Medical Education, 1968), which stated: 'people will expect treatment to be available for a variety of disabilities which in the past have been accepted to a great extent as inevitable'. Thus we see in the care of handicapped children a searching towards a higher quality of survival, just as in all aspects of paediatrics. In fact, many of the principles of child health practice are best exemplified in the care of the handicapped.

Conclusions

The practice of child health has become a specialized branch of medicine since Milroy's day, to which many physicians and surgeons devote their energies, and their aim is the promotion of the health and welfare of each new generation. To all of us working in paediatrics, therefore, the question of the quality of survival is all important.

I have looked at this subject from the point of view of a paediatrician, but I realize that the answers to some of our questions must be found by our colleagues in adult medical practice. Do they feel that we are succeeding in promoting the quality of survival? – or will they ask us why we are not eradicating the early stages of coronary artery disease or being more thorough in the treatment of chronic urinary disease, both major causes of disability in adult life which have their origins in childhood? And will they also ask us to do more to promote mental health and stability so that a more sensible attitude is taken by adults towards the prevention of accidents which can eradicate in a few seconds all the quality of survival we have achieved?

These major ethical issues cannot be solved by doctors alone; but we must both play our own part and also collaborate fully with others. There is a natural progression towards collaboration in the practice of child health today, because clinical work is no longer restricted to the bedside of a sick child, but embraces all the spheres of childhood activity – the home, the school and the community – as we seek to promote the physical, mental and emotional health of our children.

Doctors are not alone in considering the quality of survival. This is of interest to many sections of the community, and the intellectual side of the question was examined by the Plowden Committee (Central Advisory Council for Education, 1967). As this largely non-medical committee searched for means of promoting the quality of survival, they indicated the paediatrician's role. In this respect the report might be considered the voice of the population generally, and so the following quotations (reproduced by courtesy of the Controller, Her Majesty's Stationery Office) are especially relevant.

'These facts point the way to measures which have as yet hardly begun to be exploited for the prevention and the early detection of emotional and intellectual handicaps. Regular developmental examinations during infancy and preschool years can form the basis of an observation register ... The work of these services involves knowledge of child development and psychology, of health and disease in children, of child neurology and child psychiatry. It is therefore regrettable that this work is not more widely recognised as a branch of paediatrics. If it were, much closer links might be forged between the school health and the hospital paediatric service ... Herein lies a great opportunity to bring paediatric departments of hospitals into active collaboration with general practitioners and school doctors. In this way it would be possible to provide a continuous and coordinated health service for children, from infancy, through school years and adolescence.'

All of this seems to be sound advice and it can be wise to take notice of the opinions of the informed lay onlooker. In these lectures I have tried to put us in the position of onlookers of both the biological pattern of child health and of the historical background. We can learn much from the past, but in the light of present-day knowledge we may feel a little superior about the problems which worried Milroy with their strange sounding names, such as contagion, cachexia and scrofula. But any cynicism should be dispelled by realizing that, despite our advances in medical science, we are also still battling with intangibles such as personal attitudes and social problems. As we plan for the future we should do well to remember Milroy's advice to match advances in medical science with similar steps in benevolence and welfare.

References

Abaci, F. and Aterman, K. (1968). 'Changes of the placenta and embryo in early spontaneous abortion.' *Am. J. Obstet. Gynec.* **102**, 252

Abel-Smith, B. and Townsend, P. (1966). *The Poor and the Poorest: a new Analysis of the Ministry of Labour's 'Family Expenditure Surveys' of 1953–54 and 1960.* Occasional Papers on Social Administration, 17. London: Bell

Addison, P. H. (1968). 'Abortion Act 1967.' *Lancet* **2**, 503

Ainsworth, M. A. (1962). 'Deprivation of maternal care.' *Publ. Hlth Pap. W.H.O.* **14**, 97

Allan, J. D. and Brown, J. K. (1968). In *Some Recent Advances in Inborn Errors of Metabolism*, p. 14. Ed. by K. S. Holt and V. P. Coffey. Edinburgh and London: Livingstone

Annotation (1964). 'Assaulted children.' *Lancet* **1**, 543

Baird, D. (1945). 'The influence of social and economic factors on still births and neonatal deaths.' *J. Obstet. Gynaec. Br. Emp.* **52**, 339

Barron, S. L. (1968). 'The epidemiology of human pregnancy.' *Proc. R. Soc. Med., Symp. No. 10,* **61**, 1200

Beard, R. W. (1968). 'Foetal diagnosis.' *Proc. R. Soc. Med., Symp. No. 10,* **61**, 1247

Bergés, J. and Lézine, I. (1965). *The Imitation of Gestures.* Clinics in Developmental Medicine 18. London: Heinemann Medical

Birch, H. G. (1968). 'Health and the education of socially disadvantaged children.' *Devl Med. child Neurol.* **10**, 580

Booth, R. E., Dardarian, G. and Satterthwaite, M. (1967). *Culturally Disadvantaged.* Detroit: Wayne State Univ. Press

Bowlby, J. (1952). *Maternal Care and Mental Health.* W. H. O. Monogr. 2. Geneva: W. H. O.

Brown, R. C. (1948). *Reproduction and Survival.* London: Edward Arnold

Butler, N. R. and Bonham, D. G. (1963). *Perinatal Mortality.* Edinburgh and London: Livingstone

Castellanos, R., Aguero, O. and De Soto, E. (1968). 'Abdominal decompression.' *Am. J. Obstet. Gynec.* **100**, 924

Central Advisory Council for Education (1967). *Children and their Primary Schools.* London: H.M.S.O.

Central Health Services Council. (1967). *Child Welfare Centres. Report of Sub-committee of Standing Medical Advisory Committee.* London: H.M.S.O.

Cruz-Coke, R. (1968). 'Birth control and human evolution.' *Lancet* **2**, 1249

Darwin, C. (1859). *On the Origin of Species by means of Natural Selection.* London: Murray

Dawes, G. S. (1968). *Fetal and Neonatal Physiology.* Chicago: Year Book Med. Pub.

Dobzhansky, T. (1966). 'A geneticist's view of human equality.' *The Pharos of A.O.A.,* **29,** 12. Fulton, Missouri: Ovid Bull Press

Douglas, J. W. B. (1966). *The Home and the School.* London: MacGibbon and Kee

Drillien, C. M. (1967). In Roy. Coll. Phys. Symposium (unpublished)

Dybwad, G. (1969). *Challenges in Mental Retardation.* New York: Columbia Univ. Press

Ebbs, J. H., Brown, A., Tisdall, F. F., Moyle, W. J. and Bell, M. (1942). 'The influence of improved prenatal nutrition upon the infant.' *Can. med. Ass. J.* **46,** 6

Eckstein, H. B. and McNab, G. H. (1966). 'Myelomeningocele and hydrocephalus — the impact of modern treatment.' *Lancet* **1**, 842

Editorial (1966). 'A time to die.' *Med. J. Aust.* **2**, 710

Egan, D. (1966). 'The future role of the local health authorities in the day care of young children.' *Publ. Hlth, Lond.* **80,** 233

Forfar, J. O. (1968). 'Children's hospitals, children's departments, and hospital child health community centres.' *Lancet* **2**, 674

Forrester, R. M. (1965a). 'The child — general psychological and social aspects.' In *Proceedings of a Symposium on Spina Bifida.* Horsham, Sussex: Action for Crippled Child

— (1965b). 'Salvage.' *Lancet* **1**, 262

Gregg, N. McA. (1941). 'Congenital cataract following german measles in the mother.' *Trans. ophthal. Soc. Aust.* **3**, 35

Gruenwald, P. (1964). 'Infants of low birth weight among 5000 deliveries.' *Pediatrics, Springfield* **34**, 157

— (1967). In *Advances in Reproductive Physiology,* Vol. 2, p. 279. Ed. by A. Mclaren. London: Logos Press

— (1968). In *Aspects of Prematurity and Dysmaturity.* Ed. by J. H. P. Jonxis, H. K. A. Visser and J. A. Troelstra. Leiden, Netherlands: Stenfert Kroese

Heyns, O. S. (1959). 'Abdominal decompression in the first stage of labour.' *J. Obstet. Gynaec. Br. Emp.* **66**, 220

— (1963). *Abdominal Decompression.* Johannesberg: Witwatersrand Univ. Press

— (1965). 'Abdominal decompression: a better start to life?' *Discovery* **26**, 11

Holt, K. S. (1958a). 'Resuscitation of the newborn.' *Nurs. Times* **54**, 857

— (1958b). 'The influence of a retarded child upon family limitation.' *J. ment. Defic. Res.* **2**, 28

— (1965). *Assessment of Cerebral Palsy,* Vol. 1. London: Lloyd-Luke

— (1966a). 'Principles of child health as seen in the care of handicapped children.' *Proc. R. Soc. Med.* **59**, 135

— (1966b). 'Facts and fallacies about neuromuscular function in cerebral palsy as revealed by electromyography.' *Devl Med. child Neurol.* **8**, 255

— (1967). 'Electromyographic assessment of drug therapy in infantile cerebral palsy.' *Proc. 8th Internat. Congr. Neurol.* 231

— (1968). 'The "at risk" concept.' *Matern. Child Care* **4**, 145

— (1969). 'Language disorder. Case report.' *Proc. R. Soc. Med.* **62**, 1064

— and Reynell, J. K. (1967). *Assessment of Cerebral Palsy,* Vol. II. London: Lloyd-Luke

Hutchinson, J. (1861). 'Heredito-syphitic struma: and on the teeth as a means of diagnosis.' *Br. med. J.* **1**, 515

Illingworth, R. S. and Illingworth, C. (1965). 'Thou shalt not kill.' *Clin. Pediat.* **4**, 305

James, W. (1902). *The Varieties of Religious Experiences: a Study in Human Nature.* London: Longmans

Johnston, S. (1968). 'Two kinds of tolerance.' *Aust. paediat. J.* **4**, 194

Klopper, A. (1968). 'The assessment of feto-placental function by estriol assay.' *Obstet. Gynec. Surg.* **23**, 813

Knox, E. G. (1967). 'Spina bifida in Birmingham.' *Devl Med. child Neurol.* Suppl. **13**, 14

Laurence, K. M. and Tew, B. J. (1967). 'Follow-up of 65 survivors from the 425 cases of spina bifida born in S. Wales between 1956 and 1962.' *Devl Med. child Neurol.* Suppl. **13**, 1

Lawson, J. S. (1968). 'Ethical problems associated with the management of congenitally handicapped newborn infant.' *Aust. paediat. J.* **4**, 186

Lenz, W. (1962). 'Thalidomide and congenital abnormalities (letter).' *Lancet* **1**, 45

Lewis, T. L. T. (1969). 'The Abortion Act.' *Br. med. J.* **1**, 241

Liddicoat, R. S. (1968). 'The effects of maternal antenatal decompression treatment on infant mental development.' *S. Afr. med. J.* **42**, 203

Lilienfeld, A. M. and Pasamanick, B. (1954). 'Association of maternal and fetal factors with the development of epilepsy.' *J. Am. med. Ass.* **155**, 719

Lloyd, J. K., Wolff, O. H. and Whelan, W. S. (1961). 'Childhood obesity.' *Br. med. J.* **2**, 145

Lorber, J. (1968). 'The results of early treatment of extreme hydrocephalus.' *Devl Med. child Neurol.* Suppl. **16**, 21

— (1971). 'Results of treatment of myelomeningocele.' *Devl Med. child Neurol.* **13**, 279

McDonald, A. (1967). *Children of very low Birth Weight.* Spastics Research Monograph, 1. London: Heinemann Medical

MacKeith, R. C. (1967). 'Social consequences of the increased survival rate of people with congenital malformations.' *Matern. Child Care,* **3**, 437

— and Bax, M. (1963). *Minimal Cerebral Dysfunction.* Clinics in Developmental Medicine, 10. London: Heinemann Medical

McKeown, T. (1967). In *Social and Genetic Influences on Life and Death*. Ed. by R. Platt and A. S. Parkes. Edinburgh: Oliver & Boyd

Mathews, D. D. and Loeffler, F. E. (1968). 'The effect of abdominal decompression on fetal oxygenation during pregnancy and early labour.' *J. Obstet. Gynaec. Br. Cwlth* **75**, 268

Millen, J. W. (1962). *The Nutritional Basis of Reproduction*. Springfield: Thomas

Ministry of Social Security. (1967). *Circumstances of Families*. London: H.M.S.O.

Nachtigall, L., Barrett, M., Hogsander, U. and Levitz, M. (1968). 'Plasma estriol levels in normal and abnormal pregnancies. An index of fetal welfare.' *Am. J. Obstet. Gynec.* **101**, 638

Nayak, S. K. (1968). 'Pathology of abortion: essential abortion.' *Obstet. Gynec., N.Y.*, **32**, 316

Neale, A. V. (1964). *The Advancement of Child Health*. London: Athlone Press

Oppé, T. E. (1967). 'Risk registers for babies.' *Devl Med. child. Neurol.* **9**, 13

Park, W. W. (Ed.) (1965). *The Early Conceptus, Normal and Abnormal*. Edinburgh and London: Livingstone

Pollak, M. (1969). *M.D. Thesis*, University of London

Prechtl, H. F. R. (1967). 'Neurological sequelae of prenatal and perinatal complications.' *Br. med. J.* **4**, 763

Pringle, M. L. Kellmer (1965). *Deprivation and Education*. London: Longmans

Rapin, I., Tourk, L. M. and Costa, L. D. (1966). 'Evaluation of the Purdue Pegboard as a screening test for brain damage.' *Devl Med. child Neurol.* **8**, 45

Registrar General (1965). *Statistical Review of England and Wales, III, 41*. London: H.M.S.O.

— (1971). *Statistical Review of England and Wales, I, 5*. London: H.M.S.O.

Reynell, J. (1969). 'Developmental approach to language disorders.' *Br. J. disord. Commun.* **4**, 33

Richards, I. D. G. and Roberts, C. J. (1967). 'The "at risk" infant.' *Lancet* **2**, 711

Ritchie-Calder, Baron (1971). 'The doctor's dilemma.' *The Times* 5 June

Rogers, M. G. H. (1967). 'The "at risk" infant (letter).' *Lancet* **2**, 988

— (1968). 'Risk registers and early detection of handicaps.' *Devl Med. child Neurol.* **10**, 651

Rosenheim, M. (1968). 'Health in the world of tomorrow.' *Lancet* **2**, 821

Royal Commission on Medical Education. (1968). *Report: Cmnd. 3569*. London: H.M.S.O.

Rutter, M., Tizard, J. and Whitmore, K. (1969). *Health of the School Child*. London: H.M.S.O.

Schutt, W. H. (1969). In *Perinatal Problems*, p. 283. Ed. by N. R. Butler and E. D. Alberman. Edinburgh and London: Livingstone

Sharp, F. (1968). 'Estimation of fetal maturity by amniotic fluid exfoliative cytology.' *J. Obstet. Gynaec. Br. Cwlth* **75**, 812

Sharrard, W. J., Zachary, R. B., Lorber, J. and Bruce, A. M. (1963). 'A controlled trial of immediate and delayed closure of spina bifida cystica.' *Archs Dis. Childh.* **38**, 18

Sheridan, M. D. (1959). 'Neglectful mothers.' *Lancet* **1**, 722
— (1960). 'Vision screening of very young or handicapped children.' *Br. med. J.* **2**, 453
— (1962). 'Infants at risk of handicapping conditions.' *Mon. Bull. Minist. Hlth Lab. Serv.* **21**, 238
Shirodkar, V. N. (1967). 'Long term results with the operative treatment of habitual abortion.' *Triangle* **8**, 123
Simpson, W. J. (1957). 'A preliminary report on cigarette smoking and the incidence of prematurity.' *Am. J. Obstet. Gynec.* **73**, 808
Sims, E. B. (1968). 'To keep alive.' *Aust. paediat. J.* **4**, 193
Smithells, R. W. (1965). 'The epidemiology of spina bifida.' *Proceedings of a Symposium on Spina Bifida.* Horsham, Sussex: Action for Crippled Child
Stevenson, A. C. (1967). In *Fifth World Congress of Gynaecology and Obstetrics, Sydney*, p. 699. Ed. by C. Wood. Sydney and London: Butterworth
Stewart, W. H. (1967). 'The unmet needs of children.' *Pediatrics, Springfield* **39**, 157
Tanner, J. (1962). *Growth at Adolescence*, 2nd ed. Oxford: Blackwell
Thomas, C. E. (1968). *The Registration of Children at Risk of Handicap.* D.P.M. Dissertation, University of London
Vaughan, D. H. (1968). 'Some social factors in perinatal mortality.' *Br. J. prev. soc. Med.* **22**, 138
Villemin, J. A. (1868). *Etudes à la Tuberculose.* Paris: Baillière
Wegman, M. E. (1972). 'Annual review of vital statistics for 1969/70.' *Pediatrics, Springfield* **48**, 479
Wood, C., Lumley, J. and Renou, P. (1967). 'A clinical assessment of foetal diagnostic methods.' *J. Obstet. Gynaec. Br. Cwlth* **74**, 823
Wright, H. F. (1960). In *Handbook of Research Methods in Child Development*, p. 71. Ed. by P. H. Mussen. New York and Chichester: Wiley
Young, M. and Willmott, P. (1957). *Family and Kinship in East London.* London: Routledge & Kegan Paul
Yudkin, S. (1967). *0–5. A Report of the Care of Pre-school Children.* National Society of Children's Nurseries
— and Yudkin, G. (1968). 'Poverty and child development.' *Devl Med. child Neurol.* **10**, 569
Zachary, R. B. (1968). 'Ethical and social aspects of treatment of spina bifida.' *Lancet* **2**, 275

3 — The Need for Long-term Care

FACTORS INFLUENCING THE ADMISSION OF CHILDREN TO HOSPITALS FOR THE SUBNORMAL

Sheila Hewett, BA, PhD

Research Social Scientist
Child Development Research Unit
University of Nottingham

Contents

Foreword

The problems faced by parents of severely handicapped children in our society are at once so immediately demanding and so unremittingly persistent that they embarrass the imaginations of those who have been spared them; many otherwise good and compassionate people, both lay and professional, would prefer not to think too seriously about such matters. But the parents of handicapped children are not a group apart, *unless and until we make them so.* They are just ordinary people to whom handicap has happened; whereupon, in addition to coping with the obvious practical and economic burdens, they too often find themselves faced with a social isolation that almost amounts to stigmatization from their fellow citizens. Like the bereaved (and indeed they do grieve for the child as he might have been), they offend public taste by drawing attention to aspects of the human condition which our society finds unmentionable.

Thus the uninvolved, as they turn away, console themselves that special facilities exist for 'that sort of case' and that the authorities in their wisdom have made the necessary provisions. All that remains (and professional workers may contribute to this idea) is simply to reconcile parents, who are inevitably suffering emotional distress, to the realities of their unfortunate situation as we see it. So society piles on the final indignity by suggesting that parents of handicapped children are no longer capable of making rational judgements about what is best either for their own children or for themselves. Perhaps the time has now come for us to shift our perspectives and to ask whether society's own attitudes to such parents might not be suspect.

It is an accepted phenomenon of psychopathology that when human beings are faced with severe emotional pressure there is a tendency to resort first to denial and then to repression. We need not be very astonished that these classic defence mechanisms have their analogue in the administrative procedures which society too frequently offers to parents. In the 'denial phase', the reaction of the so-called helping professions is simply to behave as if there were no necessity to recognize the existence of a problem. In many, many areas of this country, the only helpful provision for the child's day-to-day special needs is the attendance allowance; additional help directed towards the individual child's condition, especially during the pre-school years, is apparently regarded as quite unnecessary. Parents, too, may be deliberately hindered from learning about the problems they will inevitably meet as time goes on. Later — often much later — a sudden change in official attitudes seems to occur. Instead of leaving the parents to cope unsupported, it is decided that the only possible solution is to excise the child dramatically and finally from both his family and the community. By this time, since the capacity to bear stress unsupported is not unlimited, that may indeed have become the only possible solution.

Is it beyond us to find and implement a middle course between ignoring the child and taking him over completely? Dr. Hewett's report raises some uncomfortable and pertinent questions. The most uncomfortable have to do, not with the ability of parents to cope with their handicapped children, but with the reluctance of society to share rather than extinguish their involvement.

JOHN NEWSON, BSc, PhD, and
ELIZABETH NEWSON, BA, PhD
Child Development Research Unit
University of Nottingham

Preface

The study which is described here was commissioned by the Spastics Society. The changed climate of opinion regarding the care of severely subnormal children prompted the Society to ask what were the factors related to admission to subnormality hospitals and, in particular, whether children were being admitted because of rejecting attitudes in their mothers rather than because their condition necessitated care away from home. If this were the case, preventive action might be taken which would possibly enable the children to remain, at least for a longer time if not permanently, with their own families. A regional pilot study was proposed which was intended to indicate whether research into this aspect of the care of severely subnormal children would be worthwhile, using a national sample.

It was decided to limit the geographical and administrative areas concerned to Nottinghamshire and Leicestershire for the following reasons: the two counties were within a reasonable distance from Nottingham; they were not too dissimilar with regard to size and distribution of population; they both included rural and farming communities as well as a prosperous industrial city; the time limit set (October 1968 to September 1970) precluded wider coverage by one worker.

The sample was, at the request of the Society, to be confined to severely subnormal children* with additional handicaps, and all children with Down's syndrome were to be excluded. Mothers of children admitted to hospital and of children being cared for in the community were to be interviewed using techniques which had been employed with the sample of mothers of cerebral palsied children previously investigated for the Society.

This work was undertaken with the help and co-operation of Dr. H. Hunter of Balderton Hospital, Newark, Dr. A. A. Valentine of Glenfrith Hospital, Leicester, Dr. A. R. Buchan, County Medical Officer for Leicestershire, and Dr. W. H. Parry, Medical Officer of Health for Nottingham. I am very much indebted to them. The interviewing of mothers was completed between May 1969 and May 1970. I am also indebted to John and Elizabeth Newson, Joint Directors of the Child Development Research Unit, University of Nottingham, for allowing me once more to use some of their questions on child rearing and for their encouragement and support while the work was being carried out in their Unit.

SHEILA HEWETT

*Aged from 5 to 16 years, inclusive

A Note on Research Findings and Methods

There is no lack of literature concerning the impact of the mentally handicapped child on his family. Much of it is written by and for social workers, and concerns the 'counselling' of such families. The assumption (not in itself an unreasonable one) is that the arrival of a mentally handicapped child will create problems for his family and that they will need help to deal with these problems. Less reasonable is the generally held belief that both parents and siblings will develop undesirable or pathological attitudes towards the handicapped child, most commonly that the child will suffer 'rejection' by his mother. It is unusual to find the contentions of these writers supported by reference to research findings and there is considerable variation in the quality of their arguments. Some scarcely rise above the level of after-dinner conversation (Michaels and Schucman, 1962) while others are careful and thoughtful discussions of the issues involved (Baum, 1962; Dittman, 1962; Stone, 1967). Generalizations are made from case studies of small numbers of highly selected families (Grebler, 1952; Peck and Stevens, 1960), but there is a marked lack of any precise definition of the terms used. One outstanding exception is an article by Gallagher (1956) in which he not only defines 'rejection' but also describes ways in which rejecting feelings may be expressed. He cautions social workers and other professionals against the careless use of the word and advises them to examine their own feelings and motives before making judgements about the families they hope to help, pointing out that the labelling process may in fact hinder, rather than facilitate, the counselling process. However, in 1963 Erikson still found it necessary to comment that '. . . our occupational prejudice is the rejecting mother'. In the same year, Roith (1963) attempted to bring some perspective to the problem in a paper entitled 'The myth of parental attitudes'. He had been led by his reading of the literature to expect 'hordes of guilty and rejecting parents to descend' on him, since he was a psychiatrist concerned with parents of mentally handicapped children. When they did not arrive, he conducted a small survey in an effort to assess the prevalence of adverse attitudes. Unfortunately, only 60 per cent of them returned his postal questionnaire. Among this number, he found little evidence of the feelings he had expected to find − in particular, the *guilty* feelings − but we know nothing of the 40 per cent who did not reply.

Matheny and Vernick (1969) found that what parents lacked most was adequate information. The attitudes of the 40 families they studied became very positive when this lack was remedied and they, too, warned that counsellors may not do their work well if they concentrate on what they think are emotional aberrations in the parents. Psychotherapy is no substitute for information.

In spite of such efforts, however, in the White Paper *Better Services for the Mentally Handicapped* (Department of Health and Social Security, 1971) one reads that the feelings of parents 'can lead, for example, to rejection of the handicapped child . . .'. The preoccupation noted by Erikson still seems to exist.

Not surprisingly, in view of the vagueness of the concepts used, some efforts to measure parental attitudes, or to establish their presence, have come to grief. Ricci (1969) used PARI (Parental Attitude Research Instrument) in an attempt to discover whether mothers of (1) retarded, (2) emotionally disturbed, and (3) normal children differ in their attitudes to child rearing. They found that the mothers of groups 1 and 2 did not differ from those in group 3. Rather than accept this quite plausible result (Boles had reported in 1959 that mothers of cerebral palsied and of normal children both showed attitudes of rejection and guilt towards their children, according to specially designed scales), they suggested that their respondents had not obeyed instructions when completing the test. However, doubt as to the usefulness of the PARI has also been expressed by Thomas, Chess and Birch (1968), who found that it failed 'to provide a basis for differentiating idiosyncratic parental attitudes within the group'.

Farber (1959) devised a scale for measuring 'marital integration' and 'sibling role tension', and attempted to show the ways in which this was affected by the presence of a mentally handicapped child. He concluded that marital integration, as defined by his measures, remained the same whether mentally retarded girls were sent to institutions or cared for at home, but that where the child was a boy, integration was impaired by keeping him at home. Fowle (1968) attempted to use the same measures and was unable to find any differences in marital integration between families where the child was at home and those where the child had been sent to an institution. She warns of the difficulties of interpreting such scales − '. . . one can never be certain that the yielded measurements of the instruments are the equivalent of the definition of the proposed characteristics'.

There are no direct measures of attitudes. Statements concerning their presence or absence are either the result of a third party having interpreted behaviour in clinical or social work settings, using concepts derived from psychoanalytic theory, or they are the result of the application of attitude scaling techniques. In the case of the latter, the assumption is that people will reveal how they feel by ticking items on inventories of questions or statements (Thurston, 1959, 1960; Cummings, Bailey and Rie, 1966). *Ad hoc* measures have also been created. For example, in Joan McMichael's study of physically handicapped children, one of the criteria used was whether a parent had discussed his child's education with his teachers during a one-year period (McMichael, 1971). Another was whether the parents were separated or divorced. It is acknowledged by the author that the judgements are arbitrary and subjective. Nevertheless, the measure is presented as a scored scale, which gives it a spurious air of precision.

Again, the rejection reported in a study by Donoghue, Abbas and Gal (1971) was judged by the parents' failure to visit the child in hospital or to ring up or send presents.* This method of assessing rejection becomes suspect when one takes into account two other, interrelated, factors: (1) that no distinction is made between children admitted for short-term and long-term care — it is unusual for parents to visit short-term care children if, for example, they have gone away for a holiday or are ill themselves, and these are two common reasons for short-term admissions; (2) in every age group from less than 1 year to 13 years old, with one exception (7–10 years), more children were admitted for short-term than for long-term care. There must be reservations regarding the results obtained by the use of such rough and ready measures.

In addition to these difficulties of measurement, the idea of rejection as a specific act on the part of the mother really begs the question that all the initiative to accept or reject the child comes from her; it implies that she actively spurns the child, whereas it makes more sense to ask whether she has failed to become positively related or attached to her child, through some failure or hindrance of the usual process. Instead of looking for the presence of negative feelings which are notoriously hard to define and measure, perhaps it might be more interesting to see whether there has been any failure to establish positive feelings. Could it be that circumstances have prevented or hindered the normal processes of establishing attachment? Or could it be that handicap is preventing the baby from playing his part?

Schaffer and Emerson (1964) have pointed out that specific attachments do not occur in normal infants until they reach approximately 7 months of age. At or after this age attachment will occur, even to people who have not taken part in the routine care of the child during the previous 7 months. Before the age of 7 months, the amount of social stimulation is important. It seems that if this is seriously lacking, the baby's ability to become 'attached' later on is impaired. This raises questions about the effects on handicapped children when they have had to spend their earliest weeks, and sometimes months, in incubators or in hospital. Are they only able to form attachments for people who have been part of their earliest social experience? Do handicapped babies with intellectual and sensory impairment have special difficulties? — this could be the case if attachment formation is related more closely to developmental levels than to chronological age.

*The use of this criterion is not stated in the paper, but is a personal communication from one of the authors, A. K. Abbas.

Some slight indication that this might be so comes from an American study (Caldwell *et al.*, 1970) which compared 18 children who attended a day-centre away from home from the age of 1 year, with 23 similar children who had stayed at home. At the age of 30 months, there was 'a definite suggestion that the better developed infants tend to be more strongly attached to their mothers'. There was, however, no difference in the strength of mothers' attachment to the infants.

Cashdan and Jeffree (1966; Jeffree and Cashdan, 1971), on the other hand, believe they have measured a lack of positive affection in 28 mothers of severely subnormal children, as compared with 28 mothers of normal children matched for sex, mental age and socio-economic grouping. They admit that this could partly result from the handicapped children's own inability to respond to mothering but conclude that the handicapped are in danger of being rejected.

If, because of early hospitalization and/or his own handicaps, the baby is unable to respond and become attached, what are the consequences for the parents, the mother in particular? Erikson (1963), for example, speaking of a child who had been diagnosed as schizophrenic, has said, 'The role which "maternal rejection" or special circumstances of abandonment play in such cases ... is debatable. I think that one should consider that these children may very early and subtly fail to return the mother's glance, smile and touch. An initial reserve which makes the mother, in turn, unwittingly withdraw.' (reproduced by courtesy of the author and publishers).

Thomas, Chess and Birch (1968), reporting their prospective study of 141 children studied over 6 years from the age of about 2–3 months, suggested that whatever the parents' expressed attitudes are and whatever their views on how to deal with the child, in practice individual children alter parents' behaviour. When children prove 'difficult', they argue that the mother's consequent feelings of guilt, anxiety and helplessness arise from a belief that, if you are a loving, accepting mother, you child will be 'good'. If your child is 'bad', it must therefore follow that you are the opposite kind of mother, that is, a rejecting mother. Throughout this work, the authors emphasize the importance of the child's responses to the mother.

Considerations such as these suggested that, rather than attempt yet another measure of 'rejection', the present study should include an attempt to discover whether some handicapped children succeed better than others in reinforcing their mothers and rewarding them for their mothering. Comparison of two groups of similarly multihandicapped children, one group being in long-term hospital care and the other being cared for at home, might show the relative importance of the mother–child relationship in the complex circumstances which antedate the admission of the child to hospital for long-term care. The ideal method would have been to study families prospectively. Gräliker, Koch and Henderson (1965) were able to do so and found no significant differences between their two groups on socio-economic status, religion, educational level of parents, age of parents at time of birth and size of family. Significant factors associated with admission to an institution were birth order (firstborn more likely to be institutionalized than lastborn children), the presence of emotional problems in the family before the handicapped child's birth, congenital cerebral defect and greater degree of retardation.

The present study had to be retrospective, with the attendant disadvantages of this approach. The interview technique described in *The Family and the Handicapped Child* (Hewett, 1970) was used. The guided interview schedule is not reproduced here, since it was intended to be used only as a 'pilot' instrument. It could, however, be made available upon application to the author.

Origins and Final Constitution of the Samples

Two hospitals and two local authorities agreed to co-operate in this research. In Leicestershire these were Glenfrith Hospital (catchment area being Leicestershire, Rutlandshire and Leicester City) and Leicestershire County Health Department; in Nottingham, Balderton Hospital (catchment area being Nottinghamshire and Nottingham City) and the City of Nottingham Health Department. The hospitals allowed me to visit wards and to search files. The local authority medical officers and mental welfare departments supplied me with lists of names of children who met the criteria of age and handicap described on p. 63. It will be less confusing to the reader if these four sources and the samples they eventually yielded are discussed separately, although subsequently, for the purpose of comparison, the samples are combined into one 'hospital' and one 'home' sample. The original plan to compare the two areas had to be abandoned — numbers were too small and probably unrepresentative in one of the areas.

GLENFRITH HOSPITAL, LEICESTER, STRETTON HALL ANNEXE AND LEICESTERSHIRE

Following my original intention to interview mothers of multihandicapped children who had been in hospital for at least 1 year but not more than 2 years, I searched the files and compiled a list of such children in Stretton Hall Hospital. This consisted of 2 children only. Clearly, admission rates in Leicester for children who met the criteria were so slow that my hope of an element of immediacy and relevance to the contemporary state of affairs in the area had to be partially abandoned. In order to obtain anything like a reasonable number of children, I had to include some who were admitted as long ago as 1964. There were 17 children on this list; 6 of them were not interviewed for the following reasons:

mother refused to be interviewed	2
mother was undergoing psychiatric treatment	2
mother had parted from the father and had moved out of the area	1
child had been admitted from other residential care, thus making his total time in residential care too long for inclusion	1

Thus, there remained only 11 children with multiple handicaps, obtained from this source. I therefore decided to include an equal number of children who did not have additional physical handicaps. There were, in fact, exactly 11 children in the other two children's wards, at Glenfrith Hospital, who met the admission criteria. However, 1 of these had been admitted from the care of the local authority and was therefore ineligible. Of the remainder:

failed to contact the mother	1
failed to contact the mother, but a neighbour said the mother had left home more than a year before	1
the parents were interviewed but the child proved to be mongol	2
(of these 2, 1 had been admitted to hospital only because the mother had died)	

Thus, in all, 17 mothers with children in hospital were successfully interviewed in Leicester/Leicestershire.

The Leicestershire Mental Welfare Department supplied a list of 65 names of children between 5 and 16 years old living at home who were severely subnormal and had an additional handicap. These handicaps were briefly described on the list — for example, 'cerebral palsy', 'brain damage', 'epilepsy'. These descriptions ranged from 'non-ambulant' to 'gait' and 'deformed thumb', so that, although somewhat rudimentary, the classifications were extremely useful because they enabled me to select the sample most likely to be as handicapped as the hospital sample. All the most severely handicapped were contacted first and then children were selected in an *ad hoc* fashion so that children of all ages and at least one example each of hearing loss, defective vision and epilepsy were represented. If a child were also described as having cerebral palsy plus a sensory defect, this child would be chosen rather than one not so described. Children with minimal additional handicaps (such as a deformed thumb) were not included. Six of the mothers so contacted refused an interview, one because she was herself a day-patient at a psychiatric hospital, so that ultimately 18 interviews were successfully completed using the Mental Health Department list.

It had been intended to include a group of children who were on waiting lists for admission to hospital. Glenfrith Hospital was able to show me such a list but the Medical Superintendent was at pains to point out that there was no absolute order of priority from this list, the situation could change for any child at any time and true emergencies took priority over children listed. Some, of course, were listed simply as a long-term insurance policy. Six children, who met the criteria, were selected from this list and were successfully interviewed.

BALDERTON HOSPITAL AND WESTDALE ANNEXE AND NOTTINGHAM

Problems at Balderton were similar to those met at Glenfrith. In a ward caring for 39 children with multiple handicaps, 9 met the criteria age, multiple handicap and length of admission. Four of the mothers refused to be interviewed (1 because she was a widow with other children and worked full-time), 1 mother was in psychiatric care herself and 2 of the children had been in the previous East Midlands cerebral palsy sample. Experience of such mothers in Leicester had shown that second interviews were very distorted because the first interview had covered some of the same ground and so these were excluded in Nottingham. Some of the questions relevant to this work can be answered from the old cerebral palsy sample schedules and it will be interesting to do this later. Only 2 mothers from this ward were successfully interviewed. At the Westdale Annexe there were 4 children who met the three criteria. Of these, 1 mother refused to be interviewed, 1 was seen but the child proved to be ineligible, having been transferred from a long stay in another hospital, 1 mother refused indirectly by never being able to keep interview appointments and only 1 was successfully interviewed. Thus, a total of 3 usable interviews with mothers of multihandi-capped children was obtained from Balderton Hospital.

As in Leicester, it was decided to include children from other wards, taking children who had been admitted in 1968 and 1969. Children who had been admitted for 1 year only (3), for 6-month periods of assessment (1) and for short-term care were not included, nor were children whose homes were in other counties. One child had been in the earlier East Midlands cerebral palsy sample and so was excluded. Of the remaining 12 children, 7 mothers were selected, of whom 2 refused to be interviewed, 2 could not be contacted and 3 were successfully interviewed. Thus a total of 6 usable interviews were obtained from Balderton Hospital.

The City of Nottingham Mental Welfare Department supplied me with a list of 13 children known to have multiple handicaps. Four of these were in the former cerebral palsy sample, 1 had left the district and 2 had been admitted to hospital by the time the mother was interviewed and so were included in the hospital sample. Of the remaining 6, 2 mothers refused to be interviewed and 4 were successfully interviewed.

A total of 15 mothers, 20 per cent of the 75 approached, refused to be interviewed — a much higher rate than in the previous sample of cerebral palsied children. One can only speculate about the reasons for this. It could be that mothers do not want to talk about mentally subnormal children, although it remains a mystery why this should be more often the case in Nottingham and Nottinghamshire than in Leicester and Leicestershire. The fact that mothers were approached through official channels might also have had an effect, though again if is difficult to see why this should be the case more in one place than in another. In one or two instances, the effect was in the other direction — mothers said that they did not really want to talk about it, but felt they owed so much to the hospital that they could not refuse to help.

SUMMARY

The final sample totalled 51: 23 in hospital and 28 at home. It was not important that this should be representative of the whole range of mentally subnormal

TABLE 3.1

Social Class Distribution (according to the Registrar General's classification of occupations)

Social class	Hospital		Home	
1	2 ⎤		2 ⎤	
2	3 ⎬	30%	3 ⎬	28%
3 (w.c.)*	2 ⎦		2 ⎦	
3 (man.)*	13 ⎫		16 ⎫	
4	3 ⎭	70%	5 ⎭	72%
5	-		-	
	23		28	

*Social class 3, according to the Registrar General's classification, has been divided into white collar workers (w.c.) and manual workers (man.).

children, but it was important that they should be comparable with each other in terms of social class and degree of handicap. Fortunately, this was the case, as reference to Tables 3.1 and 3.2 will show, although social class 5 was not represented in either sample. The method of scoring handicaps was similar to that used for the previous sample of cerebral palsied children, described by Hewett (1970).

There were more children in the hospital sample (43 per cent) who scored over 30 than in the home sample (25 per cent), but if the cut-off point is taken at a score of 20 then the position is reversed — 43 per cent of the hospital and 57 per cent of the home children scoring over 20. The similarity of the two

TABLE 3.2

Distribution of Handicap Scores

Score	Hospital		Home	
40 and over	4 ⎫		3 ⎫	
30–39	6 ⎬	43%	4 ⎬	57%
20–29	0 ⎭		9 ⎭	
Under 20	11		12	
Too young on admission to be scored	2		not applicable	
	23		28	

samples on these measures suggests that other differences between them cannot be attributed to social class and that the influence of the severity of multiple handicap is not very great. More of the home sample (61 per cent) scored higher than the average score for the whole group than the hopsital sample (48 per cent).

There were significantly more boys than girls in the hospital sample — 74 per cent as opposed to 39 per cent in the home sample (χ^2 4.797 $p > .05$). This does not reflect the proportion of boys to girls in the total Leicestershire list, from which the home sample was mainly drawn, in which they were almost equal in numbers. However, slightly more girls than boys in the home sample had motor handicaps in addition to their mental subnormality and were therefore contacted in preference to some of the more lightly handicapped boys. No conclusions from these samples should be drawn, therefore, regarding the greater likelihood that boys will be institutionalized more readily than girls. There is evidence from other sources, however, which shows that this is in fact the case, or, to be more cautious, has been so in the past.*

---

*At Harperbury Hospital, for example, it was found that males had been admitted at an earlier age 'on the whole' than females but this included admissions that had taken place as long as 20 years ago (see Moncrieff et al., 1966; Gilderdale, 1970).

Objective Factors — Findings and Discussion

It was hypothesized that certain factors would appear more often in the sample of hospital children than in the home sample. These factors can be seen as falling into two main groups. The first group included objective factors — matters about which there can be no argument, such as the sex of the child, his position in the family, number of children in the family, mother's age when he was born and so on. The second group included subjective or 'interview' factors — matters which are interpreted by the mother and which cannot be 'objective', about which the 'truth' cannot be known by social workers, doctors and others, but which concern the individual response of each mother to certain situations. It is here that one is looking for differences between the two groups on matters that cannot be assessed objectively by an outsider but which can be brought out by interview. These two main groups of factors can be subdivided in terms of the child himself or of his family. The differences found between the two groups are summarized in Tables 3.3 and 3.4. For the sake of standardization and in order to make comparisons, the numbers are expressed as percentages, but the obvious disadvantages of using percentages when numbers are so small must be constantly borne in mind.

None of the differences between the two samples on the seven factors listed in Table 3.3 reaches statistical significance. According to Moncrieff (1966), one would expect more 'eldest' children to be admitted to hospital than youngest and it was not the case in this sample.* However, it should not be concluded too hastily that it is therefore atypical. The difference may be related to the fact that it is composed of children all under 16 years of age and Moncrieff's sample (actually Tizard's, from an earlier survey) included 'children' of all ages. More important is the fact that the present hospital and home samples do not differ significantly from each other in respect of birth order, although it would be interesting to know what significance birth order has over all recent admissions of children under 16 and how it relates to incidence of mental handicap in firstborn children.

*However, *see also* Gräliker, Koch and Henderson (1965), who found that firstborn children were significantly more likely to be admitted than lastborn, in a group studied prospectively. This group included children with Down's syndrome.

There were few families with four or more children in either sample and again the difference is negligible. This was not as had been expected.

TABLE 3.3

Objective Factors

	Hospital N = 23 (%)	Home N = 28 (%)	Percentage difference	χ^2 test
(1) Position in family:				
first child	22	43	21 ⎫	
middle child	39	21	18 ⎬ Not significant	
last child	39	29	10	
'only' child	0	7	7 ⎭	
(2) Large family (4 or more children)*	9	14	5	Not significant
(3) Mother's age at birth of child: *				
under 30 years	52	78	26 ⎫	One-third of total
30–39 years	35	18	17 ⎬	sample were 30+
40 years and over	13	4	9 ⎭	at time of birth
(4) Separated/divorced/widowed	13	4	9	Not significant
(5) Baby hospitalized (*not* for permanent care)				
before 1 month old	39	38	1 ⎫	
1–6 months old	4	7	3 ⎬ Not significant	
7–12 months old	9	4	5	
more than once during first year	17	4	13 ⎭	
(6) No regular local authority or hospital day-care provided for child	30	50	20	Not significant
(7) Serious communication difficulties or no speech	87	75	12	Not significant

*Also the case in Gräliker, Koch and Henderson, 1965.

There were proportionately twice as many 'older' mothers (over 30 years of age at time of birth) in the hospital sample, which had been expected, although this difference is not significant statistically. The proportion of 'lone' parents was also higher in the hospital sample (as had been expected), although when the two samples are combined the proportion of lone parents (about 8 per cent) is not greater than one would expect to find in a random sample of parents in this age range.

So far, nothing of significance has emerged from comparing the samples on objective 'family' factors. Early hospitalization of the baby seems to be of even less significance. It had been hypothesized that this might seriously interfere with the establishment of the mother—child relationship, so that babies separated from their mothers early and often might more readily become candidates for permanent care. The evidence does not support this hypothesis. Equal proportions of home babies and hospital babies had been kept in hospital at birth or had had to be admitted before they were 1 month old; just under 40 per cent. Only 3 of the rest had been in hospital between the ages of 1 and 6 months. Four hospital children and 1 home child had been in hospital more than once during the first year of life — a difference not statistically significant in samples of this size.

It had been confidently expected that the failure to provide adequate day-care for the severely handicapped would significantly reduce the families' ability to cope with them in their own homes. This expectation has proved not only to be unfounded in these samples but actually to be the reverse. Fewer of the home children were, in fact, having regular day-care than the hospital children had had before admission, although in some cases in the hospital sample day-care would have been a tremendous help. This cannot be explained in terms of low age of home children; they were not so young that one would not expect day-care to have been provided. Five home children aged from 10 to 16 years were among those with no day-care, 1 was 8 years old and the remaining 8 were aged from 5 to 7 years. It is by no means unusual for mentally handicapped children under 7 years to have no day-time provision made for them, particularly if they have additional handicaps.

Why, in the opinion of their mothers, was day-care not enough to keep these children out of hospital? In 2 cases the husband had deserted the mother, in 1 the mother suffered serious ill-health and in 1 the father had had a serious accident which necessitated the mother's absence from home for a long period. Hospital care could not be avoided. Other reasons were:

aggressive behaviour	4 children
child's own very poor health	1 child
nights were the problem, not the days	1 child
mother's psychiatrist recommended hospital	1 child
daily travelling unsettling for the child	2 children

One child had been in hospital virtually since birth, so the question of day-care never arose. The first mother interviewed was confused by the question and could not answer properly (the questionnaire was later modified). Of the children having behaviour problems, 2 could not be contained either in special day or boarding schools and in 1 instance the child's behaviour in the consultant's office convinced him of the need for urgent admission. Again, it seems that there were insuperable obstacles to continuing to care for these children at home. Whether a subnormality hospital was the right place for them to go is a different question, which will be discussed later.

Five mothers of children who had no or only occasional day-care, felt that regular day-care would have helped to keep the children at home longer. Three did not and again there were overriding considerations — gross hydrocephaly, a deserted mother in very poor health, and 1 mother said that night relief, rather than day relief, would have helped. One mother who thought day-care would help her 4-year-old said that the mental welfare officer had disabused her of this idea. She said, 'Yes, I asked [the mental welfare officer] if she could go to one of these day schools, you see, and she said "No, it's impossible, they wouldn't accept her, she's too bad." . . . I thought this would have been the ideal solution, but she said, "You'll still have her at the week-ends and this is when you want to be with your family, and she is not acceptable as part of the family." I mean, it was cruel, but nevertheless true.' This is one of several instances where the mothers felt that they were actively encouraged to have their children cared for away from home. One mother in the home sample who had been resisting this advice for 16 years, said, 'I find you have to fight to keep them at home — not to go into a home'.

The last factor which concerns the child and is not really open to argument is that of speech difficulty. It had been suggested to me by a mother of a handicapped child (not in this sample) that this could be the last straw that made hospitalization unavoidable. Once more, however, this factor was not operating in this sample. The majority of both the home and the hospital children either had no speech at all or had only one or two words.

The following is a summary of the relative importance of seven 'objective' factors.

(1)   Position in family — no clear difference between the samples, but the biggest difference concerns eldest children and is the reverse of what might have been expected.

(2)   Size of family — few large families in either sample, but marginally more in home sample; the reverse of expectation.

(3)   Mother's age — 2 out of 3 mothers in the combined sample were under 30 years of age at the time of the handicapped child's birth. Only 4 in the combined samples were over 40 years of age at the time of birth, possibly because mongol children had been excluded. The difference between samples was in the direction expected but the factor in general was regarded as being less important than had been expected.

(4)   'Lone' parent — the difference was in the expected direction but, again, numbers were smaller than expected.

(5)   Early hospitalization, other than permanent care — incidence equal in both samples.

(6)   Absence of day-care — more common with home sample; reverse of expectation.

(7)   Speech difficulties — a very small difference in the expected direction but more than 75 per cent of all the children had serious impairment of speech.

Subjective Factors — Findings and Discussion

The similarity between the two samples in respect of these objective factors means that the differences that were found on subjective factors are the more interesting.

TABLE 3.4

Subjective or Interview Factors

	Hospital N = 23 (%)	Home N = 28 (%)	Percentage difference	χ^2 test
A. Factors concerning the child				
1. Baby 'ill' at birth	48	32	16	Not significant. Difference in expected direction
2. 'Unrewarding baby' during first 6 months	48	25	23	Not significant. Difference in expected direction
3. Baby 'too quiet', 'too good' during first 6 months	26	14	12	Not significant. Difference in expected direction
4. Baby 'seemed normal' for first 6 months	35	50	15	Not significant. Difference in expected direction
5. Child poor sleeper	56	18	38	$\chi^2 = 6.66$ df 1 $p < .01$. Difference in expected direction

TABLE 3.4 *cont.*

	Hospital N = 23 (%)	Home N = 28 (%)	Percentage difference	χ^2 test
6. Child has tantrums and/or other behaviour problems	43	21	22	Not significant. Difference in expected direction
B. Factors concerning the family				
1. Father 'non-participant'	39	18 (11)	21 (27)	On second set of figures χ^2 = 4.2 df 1 $p < 0.05$. Expected direction
2. Disruption of marriage mentioned by mother	48	7	41	χ^2 = 8.97 df 1 $p < .01$. Expected direction
3. Father said to want child hospitalized	39	18	21	Not significant. Difference in expected direction
4. Mother said to want child hospitalized	35	11	24	Not significant. Difference in expected direction
5. Other relatives said to want child hospitalized	22	7	15	Not significant. Difference in expected direction
6. Mother sees adverse effect on siblings	52	18	34	χ^2 = 5.24 df 1 $p < .05$. Expected direction
7. Mother's health poor	22	4	18	Not significant. Difference in expected direction

continued overleaf

TABLE 3.4 *cont.*

	Hospital N = 23 (%)	Home N = 28 (%)	Percentage difference	χ^2 test
8. Father's health poor	26	7	19	Not significant. Difference in expected direction
C Other factors				
1. Mother knew for certain that baby was handicapped in first 3 months	30	21	9	Not significant. Difference in expected direction
2. Mother felt she had been told in 'cruel' way	13	11	2	—
3. Hopeless prognosis given when mother told	48	18	30	χ^2 = 3.97 df 1 $p < .05$
4. Hospitalization suggested by general practitioner	26	21	5	—
5. Hospitalization suggested by consultant	35	18	17	Not significant. Difference in expected direction
6. Hospitalization suggested by local authority	43	18	25	Approaches significance at .05 level

In one respect there was no ambiguity about these factors, in that all differences were in the direction expected, although in three instances they were so small that they must be discounted altogether.

The hypothesis that early and frequent separations of mother and child would significantly affect attitudes towards permanent care was not upheld. This obstacle to the establishment of a rewarding mother—child relationship can, it seems, be overcome. So, too, can the fact that one has an 'ill' baby — only 2 of the 'ill' babies in the home sample were also seen as 'unrewarding' babies. The difference between the two samples regarding 'unrewardingness' of the baby was much more definite than that regarding either hospitalization or having an 'ill' baby. However, an interesting fact concerning this factor of 'unrewardingness' emerged during coding.

Mothers were judged to see their babies as unrewarding according to how they responded to the first question on the schedule. A few examples will illustrate the point.

(1) 'Terribly good – *too* good … she didn't respond to the usual … she lay in the pram for hours … she's not my usual type of baby … she would smile but there was no light in the eyes, if you understand, not like the other babies.'

(2) 'He was just like a little dormouse, too good to be true, never woke for a feed. You'd be feeding him and he'd be fast asleep. I've even bathed him asleep. Everyone used to say, "Isn't he good" but it wasn't long before I thought he was far too good to be true and it was me that was bothering the doctor. You know how it is that some mums will never have it that there's something wrong. I really thought there was.'

(3) 'She was very mardy, you know. Well, she used to scream a lot – we couldn't get her to feed … it worried us, you know … I knew there was something the matter with her, naturally, because she didn't do nothing like an ordinary baby.'

These were all coded as 'unrewarding' babies.

In addition to the way the mother spoke of the baby, the replies to questions 2, 3 and 4 on the schedule were assumed to give some indication of the actual difficulties encountered in coping with the baby in the first few weeks of his life. Thus the baby who cried continually, was slow to feed and vomited a lot, who failed to respond with smiling at the appropriate age, would score 3 out of 3 on unrewardingness. A score of 2 out of 3 also counted as unrewarding. When these scores were compared with the answers to question 1, it was found that although about one-third of each sample was unrewarding according to score (scoring 2 or 3 out of 3), twice as many in the hospital as in the home sample were *seen* as unrewarding – 48 per cent, as opposed to 25 per cent. For some reason, some of the mothers in the home sample were better able to tolerate their admittedly difficult babies. It is possible that the father's attitude is important here. Only 1 father of the unrewarding babies in the home sample was described as a non-participant by the mother, as opposed to 5 in the hospital sample.

The only statistically significant difference between the home and the hospital children is in the degree to which they affect their parents' sleep, and proportionately three times as many hospital as home children were poor sleepers. To be kept awake at night over a long period obviously undermines one's ability to cope with daily life and this may account for the fact, already noted, that absence of day-time care for the child did not make such an important contribution to the reasons for admission as had been expected. Night-time relief might be more to the point, and a few mothers said so.

Proportionately twice as many hospital as home children were troublesome in other ways, having temper tantrums or generally behaving in ways which family and friends could not tolerate. The father of one such child (very active, and possibly autistic) described how he saw hospital as the only means of providing a 'cage' for his child, where he could do no harm and come to no harm. He had considered, he said, the possibility of making such a 'cage', a special room in a kind of summer-house in the garden, but rejected the idea because of the terrible loneliness for the child for long periods of the day. The best thing provided by the hospital, he thought, was companionship while in the cage.

The picture, then, of the children who were hospitalized, is one of children difficult to deal with from birth or soon after, children who respond poorly to mothering and who disturb the rest of the family day and night, more frequently than is the case with children kept at home.

However, it is obvious that it is not only the kind of child that influences admission. The kind of family he belongs to is important, too – in particular, the kind of father and husband the family has.

Reference has already been made to one difference in father participation that was found between the samples. Reference to Table 3.4 will show that there are two sets of figures for this factor in the 'Home' column. This is because 2 of the fathers who scored low on participation in caring for the child only did so because of their long hours of work – both were concerned with catering. One of them had a very physically handicapped child and felt that his inability to spend more time helping his wife meant that permanent care would shortly become unavoidable. When these two fathers are not counted as non-participant, the difference between the samples reaches statistical significance.

The two other family factors which reach significance are as follows.

(1)   Mothers' reports that their marriages are seriously threatened by the presence of the handicapped child.

(2)   Mothers' reports that the other children in the family are adversely affected by the handicapped child and/or the general disruption of family life. It may sound trite and obvious to say that fathers are important, but it is not always realized, perhaps, that confidence in a husband who is supportive, psychologically and/or practically, can make all the difference between mothers and families that can cope well with serious problems and those that cannot. There are, of course, situations where even a united husband and wife cannot cope, but that is another matter. A mother who felt that her own attitude had been completely changed by her husband's ability to accept their child, had this to say when she was asked if she thought it might one day be impossible to go on looking after her son: 'Well, I don't know – the state the hospital's in at the moment, I shouldn't like to think of him going. When I first knew [about the handicap], I wouldn't have minded. I didn't want him when I first knew – I shunned him in a way ...' [*Interviewer:* 'What do you think helped you to get over this feeling?] 'I think it was my husband, really, because he sort of made a fuss of him and I thought, "Well, if *he* can, I shall have to".'

The mother mentioned earlier who said she had had to fight to keep her child at home said, 'The most important of all is, have you got a husband who'll help you? That is the main thing. You've got to have a husband who'll meet you half-way.'

What if the husband has not the kind of personality that can withstand the pressures of living with handicap? One (hospital sample) mother said of her highly participant husband, who had initially been against permanent care, 'He thinks the world of —— but he used to say he dreaded coming home, he never knew what he'd got to face when he came home. And it aged him a lot, the worry of what he'd got to do. I'd get worked up and he was tired and things got very strained. He's not a man who goes out − he'd never think of going out without me but he used to say 'I hate coming home, I'd rather stop at work".'

In another (hospital sample) family where the mother felt she had reached the end of her resources, she said, 'My husband started to go out at night, because of —— I think. He said, "I can't go to work all day and come home and listen to him screaming all evening, I can't stand it." And in my opinion he never thought of me having to go through it all day and all night. He used to go down and sit in his Mum's and then come back. Then we started arguing and in the end I knew if I didn't get away from that house − because I hated it by then and everything else, including my husband − I'd just crack up.' It is sometimes said that older, middle-aged mothers find the strain too much for them, but this was a very young mother; her second child, the sample child, was born when she was only 20 years old, her husband being 2 years older. It may be that in some ways very young parents, still in the process of maturing and of settling down into marriage, may be more vulnerable than are older, more experienced parents who have a well established relationship (see Moncrieff et al., 1966, pp. 22 and 79).

The adverse effect on siblings was sometimes something that parents worried about and was in some cases sufficiently marked for the child to be attending a child guidance clinic. In some families, one sibling was affected more than the rest. For example, a sample child who was considered to have a very successful Holter valve operating, suddenly had a severe epileptic seizure while at a birthday party with his brother. For some time after this, the brother refused to go out to parties because he thought the same thing would happen to him. Children at school had said, 'Your brother's mad', which did not help, and the teacher had noticed his school work was affected so that he was eventually referred to the child guidance service. The third child, however, a little girl, did not seem to be disturbed, because she could not remember what her brother had been like when he was well. The mother felt that as she had always known him as he was, she simply accepted him in a way that the older child could not.

As in this instance, it was not uncommon for the mother to single out older, rather than younger, siblings when talking about this problem (Farber, 1959). However, far more marked was the relationship between the effect on the children and general disruption of the marriage. Of the 12 instances of adverse effect on siblings in the hospital sample, 8 also stressed the unsettled state of their marriage. (Some of these marriages, it should be noted, were already shaky before the advent of the handicapped child, on the mothers' own admission. It is possible that others were, too, and that the handicapped child increased the strains beyond tolerable limits). In the home sample, none of the 5 mothers who said that siblings were affected said that their marriages were unsettled, and the types of disturbance mentioned tended to be relatively trivial. When the parents are able to deal with the situation, the siblings appear to have a good chance of doing so, too — the relationship between the handicapped child and disturbance of the siblings is not necessarily a simple and direct one.

It had been expected that the parents of the hospital children would say more often that their health was poor than would the home parents and this was indeed the case.* Only 1 mother in the home sample said that she did not think she was in fairly good health — she suffered from 'chronic bronchial catarrh' and was losing weight. Two others in the home sample said their husbands' health was not good; one had had a 'nervous breakdown' but recovered, the other had had thrombophlebitis but this had not apparently prevented his giving considerable help in looking after his severely handicapped daughter.

Five mothers in the hospital sample and 6 fathers were described as having poor health. Two of the mothers suffered from permanent conditions which were serious enough to provide sufficient justification for the child's admission and a third had needed psychiatric treatment, during which the psychiatrist had recommended admission of the child. One had only a minor health problem but her husband had a chronic condition of his back and legs. Of the other 5 fathers, 1 had suffered severe head injuries, 2 were described as highly strung, nervy, 'chesty' and with 'ulcers', and 1 had had serious hypertension for a number of years. In only 1 instance had the father's ill-health led directly to the child's admission; this was the father with head injuries, who had been involved in an accident a long way from his home.

*Moncrieff (1966) reminds us that in Tizard's sample from which she worked, the mental and physical health of the mother was one of the most important factors affecting admission for residential care.

Other Factors — Findings and Discussion

Families do not operate in a social vacuum. They are subjected to a number of pressures from agencies other than themselves. They are given advice, sometimes bluntly, by their in-laws, by the doctors with whom they come into contact and by social workers or other local authority personnel. It has been suggested that it is not always *what* they are told but when or how they are given information about their children that will most influence their subsequent attitudes and actions. For example, it is said that if the mother knows 'too soon' that her baby is never going to be normal, she will inevitably reject the child. This belief may be one of the factors that lie behind the obvious reluctance of some doctors to tell mothers what is wrong with their babies. With some conditions this cannot be avoided — spina bifida is the one that springs to mind, since it is known and obvious at birth to both mother and doctor. Mongolism, however, which is also usually recognizable at birth to the doctor, is not so obvious to all mothers and there may be considerable delay in telling the mother. In a discussion of the problem in relation to neurologically impaired children (Prechtl, 1963), Mavis Gunther, an obstetrician, stated, 'If you rush from the labour ward to a mother and tell her "You've just had a mongol", that child is absolutely certain to go straight to an institution'. This is an extreme, and no doubt somewhat ill-considered, statement which the speaker would probably, on reflection, wish to qualify; however, it nevertheless may well indicate what her beliefs are in general about this problem, since she goes on to say, 'But if telling the mother is put off for a few weeks, she will have developed affection for the baby and is more likely to make a job of looking after it'. This may indeed be so in some cases, but it is not simply a case of the mother's choosing whether or not to care for her handicapped child. It also depends on whether there is in fact any alternative to doing so and on whether she is or is not encouraged to look for alternatives.

Few mothers in either sample said that members of the wider family had tried to influence their decisions concerning their children, but more of those in the hospital sample had relatives who thought it right that the child should be hospitalized. About one-quarter of each sample said their general practitioners had suggested that the child should be hospitalized; just over one-third of the hospital sample said that someone at consultant level had suggested it, double the proportion of the home sample; and a higher proportion still, more than 40 per cent, said that local authority agents (such as mental welfare officers) had suggested hospitalization, about 2½ times the proportion in the home sample, and this difference between the samples approaches significance at the .05 level. Only 5 mothers in the hospital sample said that no one had suggested to them that hospitalization was advisable. One of these quite frankly stated that she had herself wanted this and had refused to attempt to care for her very ill baby for longer than 3 weeks. Her relationship with her husband was not good at the time. Another said, 'I think I hated myself for wanting her to go away — I used to go and see the psychiatrist and he said that I was punishing myself for wanting her to, that I was making myself feel awful when all the while it was the best thing for her. And I think because that's what I wanted, I didn't *want* myself to want it.' This mother was only 16 years of age when her handicapped child was born; her marriage was unstable from the start and had broken down completely some time before she was interviewed. In spite of this, she had, unlike the first mother above, looked after her child for 5 years. So had 2 other young mothers in similar circumstances, 1 until her own health became very poor and the other until her marriage finally collapsed. This last mother said, 'I wouldn't say it split us up [that is, the birth of the handicapped child], but I would say it made a lot of difference. ... My husband [divorced] would rather he be at home. ... If I'd got plenty of money and was very happily married, and I could afford to get the right sort of help, I could have him all the time.' She also said, 'I don't feel guilty because of having him. I feel guilty for where he is.'

In the other three instances where mothers had not previously been advised to accept hospital care, circumstances had arisen which made admission imperative.

This sample in fact yielded no instances where being told early about the child's handicap appeared to have any real influence on whether or not a child was subsequently admitted to hospital. Less than one-third of the hospital and less than one-quarter of the home sample said they knew for certain what was wrong before the child was 3 months old. The difference between the samples was negligible. Nor was it possible to discriminate between them on the question of *how* they were told. Almost equally small proportions in each sample felt they had been told in blunt or cruel terms.

However, there was a significant difference between the samples regarding *what* they were told. The proportion of mothers in the hospital sample who had been given a prognosis in terms which they saw as truly hopeless was more than 2½ times as great as that in the home sample and this difference was significant at the .05 level. All but 2 of these 11 mothers in the hospital sample had had this experience when the child was 1 year old or younger. In the home sample, 3 of the 5 children concerned were older than 1 year (these 3 were on waiting lists for admission). Two of the 5 were only a few weeks old, but it may be significant that these 2 mothers had very supportive husbands.

It is not clear how such a prognosis fairly early in the child's life affects the decision to admit the child. One interpretation would be that this is an indication that not only the mothers but the professionals, too, think that permanent care will become necessary. It is not simply that the mothers could make 'a job of it', as Dr. Gunther says, if given a few weeks to become fond of the child. The task is of such magnitude that no one expects them to be able to do it for long, even when they have had a period of 6–12 months in which to develop affection for the child. In some instances it is certain that other factors were more important – the total breakdown of the mother's health or of the marriage, for example, or even both these circumstances together. In other instances the prediction that the child would never improve was accompanied, according to the mothers, by firm advice to seek hospitalization of the child as soon as possible. There was no choice, either, where the child had such gross hydrocephaly that it required at least two people to handle him at all times.

In all, 78 per cent of the mothers in the hospital sample felt that they had been encouraged to seek permanent care for their children, either by a doctor or a mental welfare officer.

This by no means helped all of them to become reconciled to their decision. It is sometimes suggested that permanent care solves all the problems of the parents and family of the handicapped child and that parents gladly relinquish their responsibilities. This is not so. There is evidence from this hospital sample that to have sent the child away, even when it was quite unavoidable, continues to cause pain to more than 80 per cent of the parents (Dittman, 1962). (This can have the effect of reducing the frequency of visiting the child, too, although this is also much affected by the sheer practical difficulties of getting to the hospital and by the fact that some parents get the impression that frequent visiting is not welcomed by the staff at the hospitals.) Some of their comments, below, illustrate how very mixed their feelings are, even when they say that they think the hospital is a 'very nice' place.

(1) Admission age 7 years. — 'People say "He's in the best place; he's much better off there", but I wonder whether he is or he isn't. I know I couldn't cope with him as he was getting, but I don't think anybody likes to think they can't do it.'

(2) Admission age 4 (?) years. — 'You feel guilty because you let them go away; well, *I* do, I feel awful about it but I can't cope. I've tried and tried and that's it. Well, I blame myself a lot because I couldn't cope. . . . I told my own doctor how I felt when —— had gone [into hospital] and he said I was being silly because I'd got two other children to think about as well. There was nothing that could be done and I just had to accept it. . . . We didn't want it to happen. We knew if it didn't our marriage would split up and that would be it. My husband took her in. I know he broke down at the hospital and he sat talking to the sister in the office for quite a while. . .I wondered where he was. And his brother came in and said "Frank's in —— Park. He's sat on the grass crying and he's got a bottle of whisky." And I couldn't believe it because he likes a drink like any man but he doesn't drink like that. So I went down there and he was just blotto; he didn't know what he was doing.'

(3) Admission age 5 years. — 'Well, it hurts when you go up [to the hospital to visit] and you know that you don't do anything for him. They're looking after something that belongs to you, sort of thing. You feel cut off altogether — well, I do now. But I think you accept it because he's not a normal child who's going to get better; I suppose that's what it is.'

(4) Admission age 4 years. — 'Well, I felt so ill myself, I really did, I knew I was beginning to break up, but I don't think you like to admit it to yourself;

and, it may sound silly, but I've never forgiven myself for letting her go away. I think when they go to a place like this, they don't sort of belong to you any more. They belong to someone else. I mean, she doesn't even know us now. I didn't really have any choice, I suppose; only to let her go. I don't think we'll ever solve it, because no two people feel the same about it, you know. Me and my husband don't, anyway. He said "Oh, she's in the finest place", and that's more or less where it stops, but I think a woman's feelings are entirely different.' When this mother went to her doctor to tell him how she felt depressed most of the time, he 'told her off' and said, 'If you'd come while —— was at home, well then I could have understood it, but not now'. The child had been in hospital for 4 years. Perhaps it is not sufficiently understood that permanent care does not solve all the problems.

Admission or Community Care — Some Implications for the Family

If parents do not really want their children to go to subnormality hospitals and if medical and other authorities believe they are better off elsewhere, what more could be done to prevent admission? The mothers themselves gave the answers listed in Table 3.5

TABLE 3.5

Kind of help	No. of mothers
Day-care	3
Social work visits, or someone to talk to them and explain things	3
Help in the house or other practical help	6
Day-nursery for sibling	1
Nothing	11
	24*

*One mother appears in two categories.

However, even though some mothers thought help could have been given to prevent admission, this would probably have only meant postponement of the inevitable. More than half the home sample (17 out of 28) also thought that hospital would be inevitable at some future date, 6 of these children already being on waiting lists. Most of the severely handicapped children were expected to become too big to handle when they reached their teens and parents were becoming older. The only mother of a *severely* handicapped child who could not foresee a time when it would no longer be possible to care for her at home, did not expect the child to live very long. This mother provides a good example of how some mothers of very severely handicapped children cope almost entirely unaided. She lives in an area where there is no suitable day-time provision for a partially sighted, non-ambulant, incontinent, severely subnormal 10-year-old. A 6-week period of attendance at a subnormality hospital for 2 days a week had not worked out well. The child was tipped out of her wheelchair by some of the more active children. She cried every night when she got home and seemed exhausted, so the mother felt it was not helping her or the child. The only other practical help she had was the provision of disposable nappies and she had heard of these through another mother, not through either of the social work agencies who had visited her. Of these visitors, she said, 'Well, they just come to see if you're treating them all right, you know. I must admit, they don't give you too much information — like these nappy pads — I should have found out about them years ago.' She also said, 'I've had ten years looking after a baby and I might have another ten', but no one had suggested to her that it might be a good idea to try to arrange permanent care for some future date, nor that a period of short-term care would help. Her short contacts with the hospital, when taking the child for day-care, had made her absolutely determined that she would never go there to be cared for, whatever the circumstances. This baby had been a normal child until she contracted meningitis at the age of 17 months, so one could argue that the mother's devotion to her could be due to the normal relationship which had been well established before the illness. But this is too simple. Describing the change in the child when she came out of hospital, the mother herself said, 'She recognized me right up till she went in a coma and that was it. It was like having a new wee baby really. I mean —— *died and I brought out somebody else.* ... When I brought her home, she couldn't move her eyes or open her mouth or her hands. She was just a block of wood. She was nothing. She had no expression, she never made a noise for nearly two months.' This mother could not pick up the threads of the old relationship with her child. She had to recreate a relationship with a child who had been absent from her in hospital for four months and had come home a stranger. She had certainly managed this difficult task but at some cost to herself. She had decided to devote all her time to the two children she had instead of having a family of four, as she had planned. She also felt that the developmental cycle of the family had been arrested, as described by Farber (1959), in a way which she had not foreseen when she embarked on the care of her handicapped child. 'You've *always* got this baby with you. Life

89

doesn't change so quick for the likes of us. You can't see them grow up. I look at [other familes] and think, "You'll be all right — another five years and yours will be at school". We often say in a few more years *we'll* be stuck in ... It's ten years out of my life.' She and her husband were prepared to accept this, partly because they felt the child's life would be short and partly because they totally rejected the alternative of hospitalization; but it may become increasingly difficult for such parents to do so in the future. More and more parents now seem to expect to have only two children early in their marriages and to have many years of relative freedom from purely parental responsibility once these children are growing up. If care outside the home is ever of such a nature that it will be seen as a positive, acceptable alternative or complement to home care, such parents may become less willing to tolerate gross distortions or arrests of the normal family pattern.

This small pilot study, limited though it is, suggests that it may be a waste of time at the present moment to launch a large-scale study of the relationship between maternal rejection of handicapped children and their subsequent institutionalization. The scarcity of permanent care places, the nature of the care provided even in the best of subnormality hospitals (and the two in the study have fewer disadvantages than most) and the inadequacy of so-called community care, all give rise to parental attitudes which have little to do with their acceptance or rejection of the retarded child himself or of the modifications which his presence will necessarily impose on the evolution of the family as a social unit.

The facts of the matter, as far as these Midland families are concerned, are: when the child's health is poor, the mother's health is poor and relationships between husband and wife are not very securely established or are ended by death or divorce, then, provided there is a place available and *provided either the consultant or, possibly more important, the mental welfare officer is also convinced that permanent care is justified,* active steps will be taken to find a hospital place for the child. The importance of the last point cannot be over-emphasized. Unless those in authority are convinced that their need is great, parents are in fact virtually powerless to effect the admission of their children to hospital. The following examples will illustrate this.

(1) 'Some doctor came from the education, about whether he'd be able to go to school ... and she asked questions and all that. I don't think we hit it off very well — she just didn't seem interested, it was just a job, sort of thing. ... It was just a matter of filling in a form and that was it. She wouldn't give me any answers that I wanted about what could be done. ... They don't seem as though they can give you a lot of information; when he [the medical superintendent of the hospital] says, "Yes, we can do something", that's about it. ... The mental welfare officers were both good in their own way but Mr. —— didn't seem as if he wanted to push — "Oh, let things take their time". Because he once talked to me about the hospital and I said, "How do you

get these children in?" And he said, "The best thing I can tell you is to pray for a bad winter." So I said, "Why?" not realizing what he meant, and he said, "If we have a bad winter, it will kill a few off and then we'll have a few vacancies." To think you've got to wait for dead men's shoes! I'm afraid it is a bit that way, there aren't the facilities.' The child was admitted at the age of 7 years.

(2)   This next mother's experience was quite different. 'The health visitor was beginning to get worried about me. She must have had a word with my doctor, because I went to see him for some reason [migraine] and he said, "This child's got to be removed from home because you're going downhill. It'll be the end if you're not careful." She was very concerned — she was of the opinion that we should have had —— 's name down from the minute she was born, from the minute we knew finally she was going to be of no use at all. . . . A doctor came from the Mental Welfare Department and he said, "This can't go on, she's much too bad to be at home". . . . I didn't want her to go, I hadn't really thought of it. I'd had words with my doctor about it; he'd suggested it but I didn't think anything would come of it. It felt like a prison but I thought, well, this is it. It's my life and I can't do much about it and we shall just have to cope. . . . I rang up to make an appointment for her to go in for a fortnight while we had a holiday and I was promptly told there was a vacancy at [hospital], would I take her there and then, that very day [that is, for permanent care].' The child was admitted at the age of 4 years.

(3)   Yet another mother interviewed had to resort to leaving her husband with the handicapped child and refusing to come back until someone understood that she could carry on no longer. She was referred to a psychiatrist who said she would have to go away. 'He asked me all kinds of questions about her and then he told me off and made me cry. Whether he'd set out to do this or not, I don't know. He made me cry by saying, "You seem to think you're the only person who's got a child like this", and all the rest of it.' This child went into permanent care a few weeks later, aged 4 years. The mother is one of those quoted earlier who described how guilty they felt that they had not been able to cope.

All three mothers had retarded children who were extremely difficult to cope with; all had just had, or were about to have, another baby at the time of admission. All of them felt their whole families were disrupted and their marriages threatened. They had so much in common and yet their problems were dealt with so differently by those in a position to give or withhold help. The only help available had to be hospitalization because there was no suitable day-time provision made for such children. As pointed out in our previous study of cerebral palsied children, the social workers are themselves in a difficult position when they cannot in fact offer the help that families need. They in turn may be forced by such circumstances into taking up positions and attitudes which are not particularly helpful. The third mother quoted above, who left her home, husband and handicapped child in an attempt to force someone to relieve her, had tried to get help and information from a number of sources. 'Our doctor [general practitioner] said he didn't know a lot about autistic children, he said it was only something that had happened since the war. She [health visitor] just couldn't do anything for us, it just seemed her hands were tied, like everyone else's were that we met. They all started off well – "We'll try and do that and that" – and they just couldn't. Yes, there was a lady came from [town], Mrs. —— I think she was called; I don't know who got in touch with her. She came and she got her in [for short-term care]. She said if I'd got to get in touch with her again I'd got to go to the Town Hall [in a different town] and see somebody there. She only came a couple of times.' [*Interviewer:* 'Was this the person who came about her being deaf?'] 'No, that was another one. I don't know any of the names at all, there were that many that came.' She works for the people at [first town above], testing the hearing. She came a couple of times to try —— 's hearing out, then we had to go to that place in [town] and they tried it out there. She was there. And then as soon as we found out she was autistic, we never saw her again. Miss —— came about a week before she went into [hospital] – I think Miss —— works for [hospital] doesn't she? She came, anyway, to tell us that —— was going into [hospital]; she was in the psychiatrist's office when he interviewed me. She's been once since —— has been in there, just to say that she's all right.'

Perhaps there was nothing more the local authority workers could do but these parents were more fortunate than others; they also had contact with someone who could be expected to have insight into both their difficulties and the child's, the child psychiatrist who diagnosed autism. 'She said some talk a lot, some talk less, but I think we were that stunned that we didn't say anything because we just couldn't understand. And the worst thing she did do, she told us the name and address of [a family with an autistic 10-year-old son]. And we went up there straight after we'd seen her and we got introduced to this little boy and the shock just knocked us over. Mind you, he was more than autistic, he has fits and something else. ... Then we wrote down to London. Every time we heard something on the wireless – you know, these research people – I'd write off to them; and every time they sent a letter back, it got back to [psychiatrist]. But she doesn't help, you see. You try and go to her for help and she's either busy or you can't see her or there's some excuse. She was no help at all.'

A difficult kind of mother? Probably, but not necessarily. Two of her children had been stillborn, one of them with spina bifida. She had one normal daughter and wanted another, so she adopted the child who eventually proved to be handicapped. She is frightened of anything to do with mental illness and mental handicap. While still shocked and feeling very inadequate to cope with a mentally handicapped child, she became pregnant again, so that her anxieties and doubts about her ability to cope were increased beyond endurance. If it had been possible for really massive supportive help to have been provided, she might gradually have become confident enough to manage both her normal children and the handicapped one. Neither she nor her husband had wanted to give up trying to care for the child. 'They look normal – you feel guilty because you let them go away.' When she was asked how she thought the hospital staff managed to cope with the problems she had found so intractable, she said, 'The nurses say they've that many to look after that they don't bother the same way as we do, because we've got them on our own all day, so they just don't take the same notice.' She might have added that nurses go off duty, that they can resign from the job if they want to, that they are not attempting to fit this child into a normal family and domestic life, that they are free of the conflicting emotions felt by parents.

Perhaps this mother would have been helped by the 'adequate counselling on both practical and emotional problems and psychiatric help where necessary for all members of the family or for those working with them', as recommended by the National Bureau for Co-operation in Child Care (1970), but while such a service does not exist (Martin and Rehin, 1969), some parents will continue to find that they have not the reserves of emotional and psychological stamina to draw upon that other families appear to have. I think it should also be remembered that the totally incapacitated, immobile child who can be cared for like a baby is in many ways more acceptable in a family than an active child of normal appearance whose behaviour is bizarre.

The truly rejecting mother is probably extremely rare. Desperate and unhappy mothers are not so rare. Mothers who manage their lives well against all odds are the rule rather than the exception, and they will probably continue to do so and to keep their children out of institutions with the minimum of help. The problem, in the short term, if the assumption is that, ideally, children should stay at home, is to identify those who cannot cope *before* they finally break down and to channel what scarce resources there are in their direction. There is no point whatever simply in labelling them 'rejecting' – the point is to clarify and understand the pressures and complexities in their lives which lie behind their apparent rejection.

In the long term, if parents of severely subnormal and multihandicapped children are offered a range of positive choices regarding the care of their children, with support and help appropriate to their personalities as well as their other circumstances, it might become reasonable to think of parental rejection as one of the main reasons why such children are institutionalized. Even where the mother behaves in ways which others see as rejecting the child, it may be more likely that she is rejecting the total situation, rather than the child himself. She sees the implications of having a totally handicapped child, like the mother who said, when telling how she had refused to take home her very ill and handicapped baby from the hospital, 'I refused because I knew what I would have to go through. . . . It broke my heart – but if I'd had to have him at home and watch him grow – it was going to seem like it didn't bother me so much.' She was

93

afraid that if she did not take her stand right at the start, her strong feelings that she could not and would not be able to cope would be underestimated and ignored.

The research by Boles (1959) into the attitudes of parents of cerebral palsied children showed that his control group of parents of normal children did not differ from the handicapped group on measures of rejection. All parents experience rejecting feelings, but this does not mean that their over-all or basic attitude is one of rejection. At one and the same time they can experience negative and positive feelings, and it is this ambivalence — which occurs in all relationships — that is so much more difficult for the parents of handicapped children to bear, than is the case for parents of normal children. This point of view is well expressed in the report mentioned above (National Bureau for Co-operation in Child Care, 1970), where it is suggested that 'There is some pressure on the parents of handicapped children to be impossibly "good", forever understanding, forbearing, self-sacrificing ... They cannot complain about their burden without feeling — and being seen by others — as "rejecting" their child.'* Perhaps the mothers of normal children can 'forgive themselves their rejecting feelings and tolerate them — it is much harder for the parents of the handicapped to do this and some may need help, particularly where the mother and father are unable to help and support each other.

An obvious source of such help is the social worker and yet, to quote the N.B.C.C.C. report once more: 'Some feelings are more acceptable than others, even to those professionally concerned. There is a readiness (i.e. among social workers — S.H.H.) to appreciate feelings of guilt and self-reproach but it seems less easy to accept parents' anger at being singled out, burdened and restricted. ... Similarly, the sense of grief and loss experienced by parents of handicapped children is little recognised.'* If this is so, this difficulty added to the shortage of mental welfare officers who have had social casework training must mean that the support which is said to be so necessary for parents cannot, with the best will in the world, be forthcoming for many of them even now.

This pilot study has been undertaken at a time when the fundamental concepts concerning provision for the mentally subnormal are under review. In addition to this fact, in both the local authority areas concerned the medical officer of health had only recently been appointed and one had already begun to improve community services for children cared for at home. He was very ready to affirm, however, that he felt that community care, however complete and supportive, was not the right solution for the most severely handicapped and that these children really ought to be in hospital. The community-based services in the second local authority area are shortly to be the subject of a large-scale research project being carried out by another body. If this had not been the case, I had intended to attempt to replicate the inquiry carried out by Jean Moncrieff

*Reproduced by courtesy of the authors and publishers.

(Moncrieff *et al.*, 1966) into the mental welfare officers' assessment of families' needs and attitudes; but, in the circumstances, this was not practicable. In the one instance, the mental welfare service has been expanded and reorganized so that not only are there different workers now in contact with the home sample, but they are also unlikely to be able to provide first-hand information about the hospital children. In the other instance, it seems more profitable to await the results of the more rigorous research project. It would certainly be unjust to lay any shortcomings in community care at the door of the newly appointed medical officers and their staffs.

However, the question of the role of the social worker in relation to families with subnormal children can be discussed in general terms and in the light of mothers' comments. The mothers in both samples gave very similar replies when asked what they thought was the main purpose of visits from the mental welfare officer. Four mothers out of the 51 in the combined sample said that they had had no contact with mental welfare officers. Just over half of the rest (26) thought that the main purpose of visits was to offer practical help or advice. However, when they were asked whether they saw their problems as mainly to do with practical things rather than with other sorts of problems that did not have practical solutions, only 6 (26 per cent) of the hospital sample emphasized practical as opposed to other problems. In the home sample, 16 (57 per cent) emphasized practical aspects. Although the proportion in the home sample is twice that in the hospital sample, the difference is not significant statistically, but it *is* in the direction that one would expect. When the mothers who said that they had both practical problems concerning the child and other sorts of problems which were harder to bear are combined with those who mentioned the 'other' problems as the main difficulty, the difference between the two samples is significant at the 1 per cent level ($\chi^2 = 8.92$ df = 1); 74 per cent of the hospital sample and 32 per cent of the home sample.

The mental welfare officers were no doubt aware that the mothers in the hospital sample were in greater need of help — these mothers reported regular and (relatively) frequent visiting far more consistently than the home sample. Twelve mothers in the hospital sample said that they had been visited 3 or more times in a year, compared with 3 mothers in the home sample. However, it appears that more frequent visiting does not necessarily mean that mothers feel that their problems are adequately understood, and this aspect of social work services needs to be studied with larger samples.

The 'other sorts of problems that were harder to bear' than the practical difficulties of day-to-day management included anxiety about the future, uncertainty about the way the child would develop, lack of knowledge about the condition and how to obtain such knowledge, anxiety about health or family problems that were not directly due to the presence of the handicapped child and difficulty in facing their own feelings about the child. Some mothers in both samples said that they had at some time felt that either the mother or (much less often) the father, might be directly or indirectly the cause of the child's condition — 22 per cent of the hospital sample and 36 per cent of the home sample.* For some, this had been experienced early on but later dismissed. For others, it remained a nagging worry, as it was for the one diabetic mother. She did not blame herself in the sense that her own negligence or shortcomings were responsible, but she did connect the handicap with her condition. Probably the majority of these parents are looking for reasons why things go wrong with a natural process; some of them are able to make quite plausible causal connections between events during pregnancy and the birth of a child with handicaps. For example, one mother said, 'I suppose it *was* my fault really. I had my finger in a machine at work when I was 3 months [pregnant] and then I had this threatened miscarriage. And they more or less said that I didn't get the shock but the baby did. The doctor said.' Another thought that the fact that she had been x-rayed several times during pregnancy might have had something to do with it.

This kind of searching for reasons and causes is surely not the same as the kind of guilt expressed by the mothers who said they wished they had not had to send their children away from home to be cared for. It lacks the element of self-reproach and the sense of failure that is expressed by this second group of mothers. After all, as one of them said, you can hardly hold yourself responsible for having such a small pelvis that a caesarian section becomes necessary after 67 hours of fruitless labour. You *can* blame yourself for not coping with your handicapped child, and some mothers do.

Few mothers can see hospitalization as a step taken expressly for the child's benefit — it is for the family's or the parents' benefit; even, it seems in some cases, actually at the expense of the handicapped child's welfare. Six mothers in the hospital sample thought their children had deteriorated since admission. All but 1 of the remainder thought there had been some improvement, although this was most often simply that the children seemed happier or had grown and 'filled out'.

Ten mothers out of the 23 in the hospital sample said that they thought hospital was not the right place for their children. One of these thought that the hospital her child was in was not, in fact, like a hospital but more like a home, so she was satisfied. The others did not criticize the hospitals. They felt that the hospitals were doing the best they could in difficult circumstances, mentioning shortage of staff, frequent staff changes, poor rates of pay, not enough individual and specialist provision to meet each child's needs. Sometimes, however, conflicting reports were made of the same hospital — for one child not enough personal attention, for another plenty of individual attention, both in the same place. Any judgements of the way their children were cared for in the hospitals were based, with one or two exceptions, on very little actual knowledge

*This difference is not statistically significant.

of what goes on in them. Almost half the mothers of hospital children said that they knew nothing of the daily routine of the wards or of the other activities of the children. Those who said they did know something of what went on had in fact only the vaguest notions; for example, that 'dinnertime was 11.30 a.m.', 'the nurses go on at 6 a.m.'; one-third knew that there was a school or a play group at the hospital. More than half the mothers in both samples said they would like to know more about the children's hospital lives. Out of 23, 21 said that they would be willing to participate in the care of their children if the hospital were near to their homes, although 2 of them emphasized that they would not feel able to do things for children other than their own. (The question put to them asked whether, if a rota of parents could be organized for this purpose, they would be willing to be included.) When, however, parents were asked whether they would like to be allowed to go in to the hospital freely and unannounced, fewer mothers thought this would be a good idea — 15 out of 23. The main doubt in the minds of the rest was that the staff would not tolerate it, it would upset the routine too much, or, in one instance, that it would be upsetting for mothers if they arrived unexpectedly and found their children in unchanged nappies or apparently uncared for in other ways. In general, however, the comments of this small sample of mothers suggest that the small community-based hostels of the 'Wessex Experiment' (Kushlick, 1965) might be welcomed in the Midlands and that there might be a considerable pool of untapped voluntary help in mothers who were themselves in good health and without other young children to tie them to the home.

For such a scheme to be feasible, the units would have to be within easy reach. Neither of the two hospitals in the present study was easily accessible to the majority of mothers in the sample. Half had cars, so that travelling was not difficult for them, but for the other half travelling difficulties (not necessarily actual distances) were a real obstacle to frequent visiting. The Leicester mothers reported that a special bus ran from that city every other Saturday, which would take them right to the hospital door, saving a walk up the hospital drive which they thought was about one mile long. However, when journeys involved travelling on two buses, considerable time and money could be spent. These difficulties were magnified when there were other children to take, or be taken care of while parents visited. Nine mothers said they visited once a fortnight or less mainly because of the difficulties in getting there. For some, however, there were other reasons for not taking advantage of the unrestricted visiting which is now, officially, allowed. It is not clear to all mothers that this is now the policy and in some instances where mothers *did* know they could visit freely, they felt that the staff did not really like this but preferred parents to visit on Saturdays (Morris, 1969). For some, the experience of seeing so many handicapped children at once is upsetting, although most become accustomed to this in time. One mother and father (both present at interview) had not become accustomed to any of it and expressed their feelings graphically: 'I'm afraid we're guilty of

97

not visiting as often as we ought but you see,when I go, I want to bring him back all the while – oh, it tears your heart out when you go there – you're upset for two or three days afterwards. It's like going to a funeral, in a way, because virtually he's – well, he is dead to all intents and purposes.' Nor is it just parents who have such feelings. Another mother, when asked whether any other members of the family ever visited the child in hospital, said, 'No no. They all went once and that was the end of it. None of them would go again. My father's never been to see her; he said he'd sooner remember her as she was then, than how she must be by now.' Like so many of the other mothers in this sample, this mother said that it was not her own child but seeing the other children that was so distressing.

Parents are sometimes criticized by staff for not visiting their children frequently enough but, before such criticisms are made, some of the points made above should be remembered. Having one's child cared for in hospital does not automatically relieve parents of all distress. In fact, it can create new stresses and conflicting emotions. Pauline Morris (1969) has suggested that visiting may also remind them of the community's failure to be able or willing to care for the child and this can affect frequency of visiting.

It is a tremendous commitment to know that for an indefinite period every week-end must be organized around a visit to hospital. The situation is quite different from that of visiting an acutely ill child in a general hospital who can confidently be expected to return to the family in the foreseeable future. It is also different from visiting a child who is going to be in hospital for some time, but who remembers and recognizes his parents and who obviously benefits from frequent contact with them. Only 8 out of 23 mothers were sure that their children recognized them when they visited, although all but 2 thought the children derived some pleasure from visits, in spite of this. Only 2 mothers thought there was any real possibility that their child might return home some day. In such circumstances, what kind of relationship can be maintained between parents and children? The children need to relate to those who care for them from day to day. What meaning can the shadowy figures, who appear from time to time to visit them, have for children with very limited understanding? In addition to these aspects of the problem, the majority of mothers (15 out of 23) felt they wanted to retain some responsibility for their children and to express this by supplying some of the children's clothes and toys, but only 2 of them thought that the children would be aware or appreciative of their own possessions.

It is difficult to sustain any sense of being important to one's child or of sharing in his care once he is entirely in the care of others, particularly when there is little contact with the medical and nursing staff who seem to have taken over one's responsibilities wholesale. Although 16 mothers said they had an opportunity to contact nurses on visiting days, some pointed out that information was often limited as the nurses changed frequently, so that they did not know the children or the parents very well. Ward sisters were more constant but not always seen as communicative. Only 6 mothers said they had seen the doctor since the child had been admitted, 3 at their own request. The others did not seem to be aware that they could ask for an appointment to see the doctor and discuss their child with him.

In addition to the feeling that one has handed over the child to other people, mothers in the sample were quite sure that this was a permanent state of affairs. Only 1 mother was quite sure that she did not regard it as permanent and even she admitted that if there were not a remarkable improvement in her son's mental health and intellectual development she hoped that he might continue to live in the hospital and be found work to do there. One other also said that if her child could learn to talk, to feed herself and take herself to the toilet − but, above all, to talk − it might be possible for her to live at home. Half of the mothers in the hospital sample (12) did not think it possible to have the children home even for a day; it was clearly impracticable for the hydrocephalic children and those whose general health was very poor. Some thought it disturbed the children's routine − including 2 who had tried it; 6 (26 per cent) had had their children home for more than the day-time and 5 (22 per cent) for days only. This makes a total of 48 per cent of children who had been home; Morris (1969) found that 28.9 per cent of children under 16 years of age had been home (it is not stated whether this was just a day-time visit or an overnight stay), and she felt that the number was small because so many of these children were multihandicapped. At least it seems that the children in this sample were not atypical in the frequency (or infrequency) of their visits home.

Final Comment

The main conclusion from this limited study must be that over-simplified approaches to the unravelling of parental attitudes to subnormal children and the meaning of institutionalization of such children, should be abandoned. There is a complex relationship between what the child needs, what the family needs, what the family wants and what is available. The relinquishing to strangers of the care of one's child, however handicapped, is probably never undertaken lightly and frequently causes distress which is very long-lasting. At the present time, it is rarely seen as a positive choice, made specifically for the well-being of the child. This may not always be the case. If ever the residential provision for such children evolves in ways that will allow a genuine sharing of responsibility between parents and other caretakers, in situations which most nearly approximate to those in a good home, parents may be able to make a genuine choice, rather than succumbing to a multiplicity of pressures, as is now the case. Meanwhile, some parents need to be relieved of their sense of failure and loss, and all need to be offered a positive relationship with the institutions which have taken over so many of their responsibilities. It may be that, in emphasizing the negative aspects of the undeniable necessity of residential care for some groups of handicapped children, we are demonstrating that we are too ready to ask more of other parents than we would be willing to ask of ourselves.

References

Baum, M. H. (1962). 'Some dynamic factors affecting family adjustment to the handicapped child.' *Except. Child* 28, 387

Boles, G. (1959). 'Personality factors in mothers of cerebral palsy children.' *Genet. Psychol. Monogr.* **59**, 159

Caldwell, B. M., Wright, C. M., Honig, A. S. and Tannenbaum, G. (1970). 'Infant day-care and attachment.' *Am. J. Orthopsychiat.* **40**, 397

Cashdan, A. and Jeffree, D. M. (1966). 'The influence of home background on the development of severely subnormal children.' *Br. J. med. Psychol.* **39**, 313

Cummings, S. T., Bailey, H. C. and Rie, H. E. (1966). 'Effects of the child's deficiency on the mother: a study of mothers of mentally retarded, chronically ill and neurotic children.' *Am. J. Orthopsychiat.* **36**, 595

Department of Health and Social Security (1971). *Better Services for the Mentally Handicapped.* Cmnd 4683. London: H.M.S.O.

Dittman, L. L. (1962). 'The family of the child in an institution.' *Am. J. ment. Defic.* **66**, 759

Donoghue, E. C., Abbas, K. A. and Gal, E. (1971). 'The age of admission to hospitals of severely subnormal children.' *J. ment. Subnormal.* **17**, 94

Erikson, E. H. (1963). *Childhood and Society.* New York: Norton; London: Hogarth

Farber, B. (1959). 'Effects of a severely retarded child on family integration.' *Monogr. Soc. Res. Child Dev.* **24** (2), serial no. 71

– (1960). 'Family organisation and crisis.' *Monogr. Soc. Res. Child Dev.* **25** (1), serial no. 75

Fowle, C. M. (1968). 'Effect of a severely retarded child on the family.' *Am. J. ment. Defic.* **73**, 468

Gallagher, J. J. (1956). 'Rejecting parents?' *Except. Child* **22**, 273

Gilderdale, S. (1970). 'Parents under strain.' *New Society* 7 May

Gräliker, B. V., Koch, R. and Henderson, R. A. (1965). 'Factors influencing placement of retarded children in a state residential institution.' *Am. J. ment. Defic.* **69**, 553

Grebler, A. M. (1952). 'Parental attitudes towards mentally retarded children.' *Am. J. ment. Defic.* **56**, 475

Hewett, S. (1970). *The Family and the Handicapped Child: a Study of Cerebral Palsied Children in their Homes.* London: Allen & Unwin

Jeffree, D. M. and Cashdan, A. (1971). 'The severely subnormal child – a second study.' *Br. J. med. Psychol.* **44**, 27

Kushlick, A. (1965). 'Community services for the mentally subnormal.' *Proc. R. Soc. Med.* **58**, 374

McMichael, Joan (1971). *Handicap – a Study of Physically Handicapped Children and Their Families.* London: Staples

Martin, F. M. and Rehin, G. F. (1969). *Towards Community Care.* Broadsheet no. 508. London: P. E. P.

Matheny, A. P. and Vernick, J. (1969). 'Parents of the mentally retarded child – emotionally overwhelmed or informationally deprived?' *J. Pediat.* **74**, 953

Michaels, J. and Schucman, H. (1962). 'Observations on the psychodynamics of parents of retarded children.' *Am. J. ment. Defic.* **66**, 568

Moncrieff, J. *et al.* (1966). *Mental Subnormality in London: a Survey of Community Care.* London: P. E. P.

Morris, P. (1969). *Put Away: a Sociological Study of Institutions for the Mentally Retarded.* London: Routledge & Kegan Paul

National Bureau for Co-operation in Child Care. (1970). *Living with Handicap: Report of a Working Party.* London: Longmans

Peck, J. R. and Stephens, W. B. (1960). 'A study of the relationships between the attitudes and behavior of parents and that of their mentally defective child.' *Am. J. ment. Defic.* **74**, 839

Prechtl, H. F. R. (1963). In *Determinants of Infant Behaviour,* Vol. 2, p. 53. Ed. by B. M. Foss. London: Methuen

Ricci, C. S. (1969). 'Analysis of child-rearing attitudes of mothers of retarded, emotionally disturbed and normal children ' *Am. J. ment. Defic.* **74**, 756

Roith, A. I. (1963). 'The myth of parental attitudes.' *J. ment. Subnormal.* **9**, 51

Schaffer, H. R. and Emerson, P. E. (1964). 'The development of social attachments in infancy.' *Monogr. Soc. Res. Child Dev.* **29** (3), serial no. 94

Stone, N. D. (1967). 'Family factors in willingness to place the mongoloid child.' *Am. J. ment. Defic.* **72**, 16

Thomas, A., Chess, S. and Birch, H. G. (1968). *Temperament and Behaviour Disorders in Children.* London: Univ. of London Press

Thurston, J. R. (1959). 'A procedure for evaluating parental attitudes towards the handicapped.' *Am. J. ment. Defic.* **64**, 148

– (1960). 'Counselling parents of the severely handicapped.' *Except. Child* **26**, 351

4 — Growing Up in Hospital

A STUDY INTO THE CARE OF SEVERELY SUBNORMAL CHILDREN

Elspeth Stephen, MA, DipEd

Principal Psychologist
Queen Mary's Hospital for Children
Carshalton, Surrey

and

Jean Robertson, BSc, DipPsychol

Principal Psychologist
Little Plumstead Hospital
Norwich, Norfolk

Contents

Foreword

This report by Miss Stephen and Miss Robertson describes a study carried out in a ward of Queen Mary's Hospital for Children, Carshalton. The hospital is a comprehensive one, serving the needs of sick children and mentally handicapped children. On the mental subnormality side the problems were formidable: 'The hospital population at the beginning of 1968 . . . consisted of approximately 24 per cent who were clearly imbeciles, 11 per cent at the bottom of the imbecile range, and 65 per cent of idiots'. Many children had multiple physical handicaps, and probably the majority suffered from complicating behavioural disorders. The hospital facilities left much to be desired since in each ward the children had the use of only two rooms, a larger dormitory and a smaller day room, with an asphalt yard outside which they shared with children in an adjacent ward. By hospital standards the wards were well staffed, usually having two or three nurses on duty for the 20 children − but in dealing with children so immature and so handicapped this is hardly sufficient. Staffing problems were exacerbated by the frequent changes in staff. These made it difficult or impossible for the children to develop attachments to particular adults, or for the adults themselves to get to know the children.

The study took place in a single ward, with a cross-section of children from the hospital; the authors and their colleagues attempted to prescribe and to put into practice, in the setting of existing hospital conditions, a regimen which might best meet the needs of the children. Progress of the children over a 3-year period was compared with the progress made by a matched group of control children who remained in other wards.

The progress made by the less severely handicapped children in the experimental ward was substantial. Using *mental age* data derived from an intelligence test as a criterion, the experimental children gained 17 months in verbal mental age in a 3-year period, as compared with only 8 months for the matched controls. In non-verbal mental age the differences were even greater: 22 months as against 10 months. Differences in play behaviour, in language and in the emotional adjustment were less striking, perhaps because the measures used to examine these were less sensitive or more unreliable.

Particular interest attaches to the progress made by the lower grade or more profoundly mentally handicapped children (IQ below 20). These constituted an alarmingly high proportion of the total hospital population. As the authors indicate, there were no great changes here. The experimental group made

105

slightly more progress than the control group, 'but the most striking feature was the limited amount of change which took place. ... this [experimental] group was of such low ability that marked changes could not reasonably be expected ... [but] there was some evidence that the experimental group achieved a better emotional adjustment than their controls.' It must be concluded that if 'success' is judged solely by progress in intellectual development, in the acquisition of personal and social skills, or of language, the new regimen was not able to do much to accelerate development in these profoundly handicapped children.

However, the most valuable feature of the present report is not the mere catalogue of test results, but the detailed description of methods used to revitalize the wards. In the Appendix, and in the text itself, the authors describe in detail the manner in which they attempted to change the ward environment and the behaviour of staff. There are many practical tips to be gained here. Not all attempts to bring about change were successful. In particular one must view with concern the large numbers of staff who continued to handle children: 89 different nursing staff on duty during the day in the 3-year period (and probably 120 or so different night nurses, as well as a large number of domestics). As the authors point out, there is a need to examine where or not the training programmes for student nurses, and the use made of nursing assistants, can be so arranged as to make staff changes much less frequent than they are today.

A study such as this raises as many questions as it answers, and indeed one of its merits is that it will cause people to think afresh about old problems. Is it sound policy to have as many profoundly retarded children in a single institution? How far is it possible to mix children of different ages and degrees of handicap? Can a more successful programme be designed for younger and more handicapped children, or does their physical and mental immaturity so limit the range of possibilities of environmental modification that there is not a great deal that can be done for them until they are older, stronger and more mature? What is the place of formal, structured activities in the curriculum of school or ward? How can we more effectively use parents and voluntary workers in all branches of hospital work? How can we train staff more effectively, and how can we keep up morale?

Of one thing at least we can be sure. An intensive and realistic study, carried out jointly by nurses, teachers and psychologists, cannot fail to help the staff in their difficult task of caring for gravely handicapped children. The job of mental nursing is often described as 'challenging' — but it is a challenge most people turn away from. To accept it, as Miss Stephen and Miss Robertson have done, is itself a contribution to the care of the mentally handicapped. It is one which staff in other hospitals would do well to take account of and to build upon.

JACK TIZARD, MA, PhD
Professor of Child Development
Institute of Education
University of London

Introduction*

The current provisions for children functioning below the intellectual level of others of their age have been discussed by Furneaux (1969). Our study is concerned with the problems of caring for severely subnormal children within the framework of the present hospital system.

The majority of severely subnormal children in residental care in Britain are looked after in hospitals for the subnormal. They frequently live in wards containing 30–40 beds and are cared for either by nurses trained in nursing the subnormal or, only too often, by untrained staff. In contrast, normal children in a similar position are housed in small groups under the supervision of trained house parents whose aim is to provide as close a substitute as possible for ordinary home life.

Tizard and his colleagues have shown that the pattern of care offered to children in hospital is very different from that given to them in 'homes'. This is true even for subnormals and the differences are not related to the size of unit (up to 40), to the staff/child ratio or to the severity of handicap. Raynes and King (1968) have shown that two patterns of care can be clearly distinguished: on which is child orientated, as in the children's home, and one which is institution orientated, as seen in hospitals.

In 1960, Tizard published the results of a study on the care of mentally handicapped children, not in the framework of a hospital, but of a small family unit. He worked on the premise that severely subnormal children have the same needs as normal children of a similar mental level, and was able to produce evidence that they benefited greatly from an environment planned on this basis.

The development of 16 children living in the Brooklands Residential Unit was compared with that of a group matched for sex, age, IQ and, as far as possible, diagnosis, living in the large wards of the parent hospital. The children were all ambulant and functioning in the imbecile range. Lyle (1960) showed that over a 2-year period the verbal mental age of the Brooklands children rose

---

*In this study we have used the terms 'imbecile' and 'idiot' rather than the terms advocated by the H.M.S.O. publication *A Glossary of Mental Disorders* because the new terms would not allow us to compare our population with that of Brooklands, on whose experiment our study was based. In our sample the imbecile children had IQs of 20–49 and the idiot children had IQs of less than 20.

on an average by 14 months as compared with 6 months for their controls. The rise in non-verbal mental age was similar for both groups. In addition to the improvement in language development, important changes in both social and emotional behaviour were observed.

The Brooklands experiment, which Tizard (1964) later described in more detail, was, among other things, to serve as a pilot scheme in which a technique of care and education could be studied. The present project is an attempt to apply the lessons which were learned and to employ the principles of treating the children according to their level of physical, mental and social development in a subnormality hospital ward. We have also looked at a group, not included by Tizard, of children with IQs below 20 who fall within the idiot range.

We hope that we can look forward to the day when family unit provisions will be greatly increased. At the same time, we believe we must recognize that for many years to come some children will be cared for in subnormality hospitals.

The study was carried out in a comprehensive children's hospital with provision for 340 severely subnormal children. The wards were 20-bedded and this in itself was a great advantage. Looking back, we feel that it would be almost impossible to introduce a regimen of the kind found in a residential nursery into a unit of 50 or more children. Each ward consisted of two main rooms in which the children ate, played and slept, a sanitary annexe, office, a kitchen in which light meals were prepared and an asphalt playground, shared with an adjoining ward. There was a school (junior training centre) in the grounds of the hospital which was run on nursery school lines. It was attended by all the imbecile (trainable) children with mental ages of about 18–24 months and over. The young imbecile group remained on the wards until they reached this level and the lower grade (idiot) children spent all their time in this way.

Our expectations for the imbecile children were based on the results of the Brooklands experiment. We expected them to learn a useful amount of speech, to learn to be independent for self-help, to learn how to behave on outings or visits home, to learn how to get on with other children and adults, and to be able to occupy themselves happily and, eventually, usefully in a sheltered environment. We did not expect them to become formally educable or to be able to live independently in the community when they grew up.

Our expectations for the lower grade children were much more limited and we did not know to what extent and in what directions we could look for improvement.

The over-all aims of the experiment were to promote the learning and happiness of the children by providing an environment suited to their mental ages (that is, run on the lines of a residential nursery) and by involving the staff, parents and voluntary workers as closely as possible in the children's lives. In addition, we wished to describe both our procedures and the children's response to them in detail.

THE GENERAL SCHEME

Twenty children were selected to cover a wide range of age and of ability.

They lived in one ward and, for the three years of the experiment, those of a sufficiently high level attended a single class in school (as opposed to being split up among a number of classes). As a result of a generous grant from the American Association for the Aid of Crippled Children, a teacher was specially appointed to the school class.

An attempt was made throughout to bring to bear a knowledge of normal child development and to increase both the stimulation the children received and the stability of their contacts with adults.

In order to evaluate the project, the progress of the experimental group was compared with that of a group of children living in other wards. To this end, 20 matched pairs were originally chosen and the children allocated at random to the experimental and control groups.

For a number of reasons it was not possible to give a full description of all the children and instead we aimed at describing the approach on the experimental ward in detail, pointing out where changes were made or new ideas introduced.

Selection of Children

It was necessary to find 20 pairs of children matched as far as possible for chronological age, mental age and mongolism/non-mongolism. They had all to be below the age of 10 years so that they would remain at the hospital throughout the experiment. Children with very poor hearing and vision, severe cerebral palsy, or who could be classified as psychotic, were excluded. When these children, together with those over the age of 10 were omitted, 116 children remained, 36 per cent of the hospital population (39 per cent were excluded because of their age, 23 per cent because of very poor hearing or vision or severe cerebral palsy and 2 per cent because of marked psychotic features).

Twenty pairs were selected from the 116 children, 10 of whom were ready to attend school, 5 who might be potential school children and 5 who were too handicapped ever to be likely to be suitable for school. A coin was tossed to decide which child in each pair should go into the experimental group and which into the control group. This decision was reversed in the case of 1 child at the request of the ward sister as the child who was to be moved into the experimental group had been with her since the age of a few months.

The chronological ages of the group finally chosen for the experimental ward ranged from 1 year 2 months to 9 years 2 months and their non-verbal mental ages from 6 months to 3 years 7 months. Nine of the children were functioning well within the imbecile range and 11 were either towards the bottom of the imbecile range or at idiot level. Imbecile (that is, high grade, or trainable) children went to school (junior training centre) if they were old enough and had IQs of about 20–50. Idiot (low grade, or untrainable) children remained in the ward if they had IQs of 20 or under. The hospital population at the beginning of 1968 (just after the end of the experiment) consisted of approximately 24 per cent who were clearly imbeciles, 11 per cent at the bottom of the imbecile range and 65 per cent of idiots. Many of the last were children excluded because of severe physical handicaps.

The composition of the severely subnormal population in the hospital may not be typical of that in other hospitals. However, Primrose's figures (1968) for the severely subnormal in Glasgow and Argyll are similar to our figures.

Family Groups

In the ward the children were divided into two groups in an attempt to create more of a 'family' atmosphere than is possible with one large group of 20. Each 'family' was to be based in one of the rooms, which meant that the maximum use was made of the space available. Because one room was larger than the other, one group had 12 children in it and the other 8. It was intended that the ward staff would work mainly in one room or the other and that as many of the daily activities as possible would be carried out within the families. It was hoped that by these measures the children would be looked after by fewer different people and have a better chance of forming a relationship with an adult. Belonging to a smaller group should make them feel more secure and give them better opportunities to get to know each other. It was also hoped that it would be easier for the staff to know the children individually and that they would find it more satisfying to be attached to a smaller number.

As a basis for dividing the children it was agreed that responsibility for caring for them physically should be spread as evenly as possible. The final division was discussed by the doctor, psychologist and charge nurse. Six children either had to be fed or could finger-feed only, 4 did not respond to regular potting and 4 did not walk. These handicaps were divided equally among the two groups. Sleeping arrangements had also to be kept in mind; because of the size of the rooms the children in the small group slept in two sets of three-tiered beds and two cots. Three children had come from the same ward and were particularly friendly. Four children in the small group and 6 in the large group were to go to school (junior training centre). Finally, the nursing staff felt that they would like more of the disturbed children, or those who tended to wander off, in the large group, because, if three nurses were on duty, two of them would be in this room.

The children remained in the same groups throughout the experiment and gradually a working pattern evolved. Mealtimes, sleeping, bathing and toileting centred around the family unit, but the children tended to regroup for play, according to both their mental level and their individual interests. This seemed reasonable in view of the wide range of their abilities. We could have avoided regrouping for play by dividing the children according to mental level, but a cross-section seemed to have many advantages and was felt to be preferable by the nursing staff. For example, the children did not all make demands for adult attention at the same time and the rivalry between the older ones was lessened. This was particularly important as the children became a good deal more adventurous and lively over the three years. The burden of physical care in terms of feeding, toileting and so on was shared and all the staff had some of the more responsive children to look after. When the brighter children were at school it was possible to give concentrated attention to the young and profoundly retarded children.

There were some problems in subdividing the ward: the senior staff still had over-all responsibility for supervising the children and for training junior staff, and when only two people were on duty there was no one free to deal with other demands arising. However, in spite of these problems we finally concluded that a subdivision of the ward worked well with this group.

RECOMMENDATIONS

A division of wards into groups should be considered, particularly those in which there are children in the imbecile range.

Note. — It was felt by the nursing staff to be an advantage to have a cross-section of children in the ward. If there were a good percentage of higher grade children in the hospital the implications might be that, as far as possible, the lower grade children should be evenly distributed among the wards. However, this would not be advised with the present population in the hospital because the ratio of higher to lower grade children is 1:3.

Staffing and Ward Regimen

The ward was the children's home. The 10 pre-school children spent all their time, and the school children more than half their time, in the ward.

In a normal family home, children are looked after by parents who are always there. One of the differences between the care of the children at home, or in foster homes, and of those in residential care is the turnover amongst the adults caring for the children.

It may be that the turnover amongst adults caring for severely subnormal children has more effect on the learning of those children than of normal children. Woodward (1963) suggested that severely subnormal children need consistent care if they are to learn and it is difficult to provide consistent care if the adults are always changing. After discussion at the beginning of the experiment, it was decided that in order to be able to generalize from our results the experimental ward would be run as the other wards in terms of nursing staff. The hospital has a nurses' training school; therefore the student nurses change wards every few weeks, in accordance with the training programme.

GENERAL

Daily programme

The following is the daily programme for the ward.

    7.30 Breakfast
    8.15 Toilet (those children who can, go by themselves; those who need help are given it)
    9.15 School children leave.
           Pre-school children play in dormitory and playroom while beds are made and nurses have lunch
  10.00 Day room cleaned; laundry and odd jobs
  10.30 Separate groups again
  11.00 Toilet
  11.45 Dinner
  12.30 Toilet
    1.00 Play in day room and dormitory
    1.20 Children go to school
    1.30 Sandwiches and preparation of bathrooms and bundles

2.00 Play in separate groups
3.00 Toilet
3.15 Play in separate groups
4.30 High tea
5.00 Bathing; TV; play in day room
6.30 to
7.00 Toilet and bed — small ones first

The day was divided into two shifts. On each shift there was either a sister or charge nurse and 2 other nurses. The others were usually a student nurse and a nursing auxiliary. The shifts overlapped between 1.30 and 2.00 p.m. From 6.00 to 8.00 p.m. there were usually 2 nurses on duty. This was a busy time when all the children were in the ward and children were being bathed; however, for part of this time some girls from the local grammar school played with the brighter ones (details of this are given in the section on 'Visitors').

At times, when all the children were in the ward, there were normally 3 staff on duty to 20 children. A night nurse looked after the children from 8.00 p.m. to 7.30 a.m.

In addition, there were two domestics who were permanent. They were encouraged to involve the children in their activities and, in allowing them to help with dusting and bed-making and so on, they helped to widen the children's experience of ordinary daily life.

Staff turnover during the experiment

The turnover of staff during the length of the experiment was broken down as follows.

(1) Number of trained staff: 11
     Average length of stay: 12—18 months
     1 sister was on the ward for the whole period of the experiment and 1 charge nurse spent 2 years on the ward

(2) Number of student nurses: 39
     9 spent less than 1 week on the ward owing to sickness, holidays and so on

(3) Number of nursing assistants: 39
     3 spent over 1 year on the ward
     8 spent less than 1 week on the ward owing to sickness, holidays and so on

Training of junior staff on the ward

The frequent turnover of the junior staff and the constant involvement of the senior staff in the care of the children made it difficult for them to give formal training. However, Sister said that, as the experiment went on, there was a considerable increase in the amount of discussion with, and explanation to, the junior staff in an effort to involve them in the experiment.

Minutes of the weekly meetings were read by the junior nurses so that they were kept informed. One of the psychologists carried out a certain amount of training of the junior staff on the play programme for the pre-school children.

The following wall charts were used as an aid to the junior staff.

(1) The vocabulary to be used for the school children.
(2) The play programme for the pre-school children.
(3) The self-help programme for all the children.

In order to make the two rooms more homelike, each was furnished with two armchairs and a settee, a piece of Reticel on the floor for the most crippled children and on the walls in each room was a large looking-glass and a blackboard. A high shelf was fitted along one wall; this was useful because it was out of reach of the small children. There was a cubicle in the larger room which was useful for storing toys and was also used by children who wanted to play by themselves sometimes. In fact, as much use as possible was made of the limited space available. The three-tiered beds were also used to divide the rooms in order to make them more homelike.

The children had access to the offices and kitchen on certain occasions, at the discretion of the senior staff.

WARD REGIMEN

The ward regimen was made as varied and stimulating as possible by the senior nursing staff, based on their knowledge of the individual children, their interests and their level of mental and social development. Within the framework of mealtimes, time for school and playtime and so on, the children were treated, as far as possible, as individuals. Every effort was made to see that they spent as little time as possible doing the same thing together or waiting to do the same thing together. For example, although they were all toileted at the end of the morning, this was not done *en bloc*. Those children who were independent were 'reminded' and those who were dependent were taken to the toilet in turn and taken back to the day room, whenever possible, by the nurses attached to his or her family group.

To quote from Sister, 'As far as possible each nurse who stayed on the ward for a reasonable length of time was associated particularly with one group or the other. This meant that during her span of duty she was the mother figure for that group ... some [staff] seemed particularly interested in the more responsive children, others were attracted by the helplessness of the very backward ones and others again seemed to establish a relationship with the children who were "the odd men out". The longer the staff stayed, the more good use could be made of these natural friendships. . . . ' The nursing and domestic staff were encouraged to allow the children to follow them around and to 'help' them so that the children's experience could be expanded as widely as possible. As well as introducing variety and stimulation, the ward should provide security for its children. 'This was helped by the fact that we were able to keep the same 20 children for the duration of the experiment . . . the programme of the day's activities, while adaptable to allow variety, was simple and regular . . . parents and 'aunties' were encouraged to be as regular as possible in their visits so that the children could learn to rely on them . . . the more intelligent children acquired a very definite sense of belonging to their group and the more mature children showed quite a sense of responsibility – at times – for the more backward ones.'

There has been criticism of 'block' treatment of children in hospital. The nursing staff made every effort to avoid this and at the same time to provide a secure background of order. There were a few rules which the children were taught to obey. Individualized treatment may cause some stress situations for staff and children as it creates more time in which the children have to be looked after and more space which has to be supervised.

DISCUSSION AND RECOMMENDATIONS

Turnover of staff is a problem in all forms of residential care (Williams, 1967) and staff turnover may be increased in hospitals where it is part of the training policy that student nurses have to be given wide experience of severely subnormal patients. This seems to overlook the point that, in training to care for long-term child patients, students need experience of long-term relationships with children.

If there are few nursing staff who can remain on the same ward, we believe it might be best to aim at providing permanent staff for the children who have most need of long-term relationships with adults. We found that it was the brighter children, the imbeciles, who responded to permanent relationships with adults and were more disturbed by frequent changes. In our experience the most heavily handicapped children with mental ages of less than 1 year seemed to need stimulation from adults, but not continuity of relationships to the same extent as the brighter children.

In spite of the frequent changes amongst the junior staff there was a homelike atmosphere in the ward, thanks to the thoughtful efforts of the sister who remained in the ward for the whole period of the experiment, and of the charge nurse who spent 2 years with the children.

In addition, it was found that the children kept very well physically and had a low incidence of fits or accidents.

On the ward the use of each room for all purposes made it possible to subdivide the ward into two family groups and also it gave more space as both rooms were used all day. We would therefore recommend that this use of both rooms should be considered for other wards where room space is limited.

By the methods described, the senior nursing staff found it was possible to apply the principles of a residential nursery to a ward. This depended, to a large extent, on all the staff having an intimate knowledge of the children, and this was difficult when the junior staff changed frequently. We tried to compensate for this by staff attending the weekly ward meetings but this did not entirely make up for changes in personnel because in order to carry out this freer regimen, not only must the staff know the children, but the children must know the staff. We found that the most difficult children to manage were those whose mental ages were between about 15 months and 2 years, who were at the stage where they had little understanding of speech and who tended to be aggressive towards others and destructive with toys. This is quite a normal stage in child development, but when it lasts for a long time or, as in the case of some children, they remain at this stage, it does present great problems for the staff. We think that the problems raised by slow development need further research.

Weekly Ward Meetings

Ward meetings were held every week and lasted for half an hour. They were attended regularly by doctors, the assistant matron, senior nursing staff, the teacher and the two psychologists responsible for the experiment. The psychologists' secretary was always present and minuted each meeting. The social worker, physiotherapist and the administrative staff attended when they saw from the minutes that they were involved. The junior nursing staff came whenever possible. The subject matter of the weekly meetings fell under three headings. Firstly, discussion of topics as they arose in setting up the ward, such as the composition of family groups, equipment, family rooms, and later on an innovation was discussed before it was adopted; for example, the introduction of grammar school girls and the setting up of the adventure playground. Secondly, once a year, when each child was reassessed, his progress was discussed at the weekly meeting. Thirdly, matters of immediate concern were brought up at the meeting; for example, a particular child, or a general problem such as 'throwing'.

It would seem useful to run ward meetings on these general lines. The minutes were useful ensuring that decisions made at the meetings were carried out and in keeping everyone informed. They also provided a valuable record of the experiment. The minutes of the meetings were discussed with the junior staff so that they were 'kept in the picture'.

Primarily, perhaps, the ward meetings helped to provide a consistent and individualized approach to the care of the children.

The support of the medical and senior nursing staff and the involvement of the psychologists in the whole research project was of importance in enabling the nursing and teaching staff to develop their careful and thoughtful approach to the children.

RECOMMENDATIONS

We should like to recommend that ward meetings of this nature to be held in hospitals for the subnormal. We think it would be useful if some of the junior nursing staff could attend.

General Approach to the Children

We know from previous work that trainable severely subnormal children benefit from and enjoy many of the activities which are usually associated with normal children of a similar mental age. The basic assumption behind our work was that these children would have similar needs and would benefit from a similar environment to normal children aged up to 4 or 5 years. The analogy serves as a useful basis to work from but cannot be pressed completely; for example, severely subnormal children 6–10 years of age are much larger and stronger than normal 2- or 3-year-olds and, as their development is slower, they stay at one stage for longer periods. Part of the aim of the present investigation was to examine the particular problems which arise while trying to provide 'suitable' experiences.

The children tended to fall into two groups – the school children with mental ages of over 18 months and those who were either too handicapped or too young to attend school, referred to for convenience as the pre-school group. Some children moved from one group to the other as they grew older and some fell on the borderline between the two, but, in practice, we found this a useful working division. The hospital school was the equivalent of a community junior training centre.

Pre-school Children

GENERAL BACKGROUND

Throughout the hospital the severely subnormal children who did not attend the school spent nearly all their time in the ward and relied almost entirely on the nursing staff for affection, attention and stimulation. Visiting was unrestricted but, except for week-ends, visitors did not play an important part in the life of most wards.

Each ward was divided into a day room and a dormitory, and there was an outside play space which could be used in fine weather. As a rule the children were not left in bed during the day unless they were ill. Physically handicapped or very young children were placed in chairs or put on the floor (perhaps in a playpen for protection). Where this was not possible they were put in prams which could be stood outside when the weather was good enough.

All these children had to be washed and dressed, and some had to be fed. If there were several who were slow and difficult feeders, mealtimes could be a lengthy and tiring affair. Many were doubly incontinent and others responded only to regular potting.

The standard of physical care was high, but there was a tendency for the environment to be geared towards providing this to the exclusion of stimulation in other areas.

There is no doubt that the wards were often understaffed, but there were periods of the day when there were opportunities for the adults to spend time with the children, playing with and talking to them. It should be possible to make toys available without radically altering the daily routine. There was often a shortage of play material, but good use was not always made of the toys which were available and these were not always appropriate, either to the children's size and strength or to their level of development. Their access to them was often limited, particularly where physical handicaps restricted monility. Many children spent a large part of their time without stimulation, either doing nothing or showing manneristic behaviour.

The individual nurse is at a disadvantage in that she receives relatively little formal instruction in child development and is not given training in ways in which to occupy children or in the use and care of play material. There is no systematized body of knowledge for her to turn to for help and, where the progress of the children is very slow, her activities must seem of little importance unless they can be related to something. A nurse's lack of involvement in play activities is often in marked contrast to her behaviour at mealtimes where the stages of feeding and the ultimate aims are relatively clear.

THE PLAY PROGRAMME

The children who did not attend school had mental ages of about 6–18 months. At least 5 of them had IQs well below 20 and showed little interest in their environment. Others who were brighter were much more active and alert, and some started school during the course of the experiment.

Basically the aim was to establish the principle of not only caring for the children's physical needs, but of stimulating their social and intellectual development as well. Children with mental ages of under 18 months have a great deal of learning to do and normal children do this by exploring their surroundings in a most detailed way. They come to find pleasure in the company of other people and develop an interest in trying to attract their attention and in communicating with them. Gradually they learn to talk and acquire a wide variety of other skills. Although many studies have been carried out with severely subnormal children of imbecile level, little has been done with the idiot group. Dr. Mary Woodward's work on Piaget's description of early development (1959) has provided us with a method of looking at their use of play material, but there were no other authors to whom we could refer. Some of the children did play readily, but others had very little drive to investigate the world around them. It seemed that special attention was needed to bring experiences to those who could not seek them out for themselves. The amount of time which it would be possible to spend with any one child was limited and therefore, with the help of the nursing staff, a list of activities appropriate to his level of development was drawn up for each member of this group. The aims were formulated as follows.

(1)   To give each child a period of individual attention so that he experienced close contact with an adult.

(2)   To provide experience of a variety of interesting materials and objects not usually available in the ward.

(3)   To stimulate his speech in the way best suited to his present needs.

(4)   To give the child a chance to enjoy and use the abilities which he already had.

(5)   To encourage him to move on to the more advanced activities which made up the next stage in his development.

(6)   If he was not yet ambulant, to encourage progress in this area. The physiotherapists gave us a good deal of help and advice about encouraging the children who could not walk. Not all children can become fully independent, but it is a great help if they can be taught to crawl or even to shuffle across the floor.

In order to help the adults to keep the needs of each individual child in mind, these activities were put together in the form of a 'play programme'. Making some form of a time-table helped to ensure that each child had his share of attention; it is very easy to concentrate on the active, demanding children in preference to those who make very little response. It helped a nurse coming to the ward for the first time to become acquainted with the group and helped to emphasize the need for getting out the play material and taking care of it and of not leaving the children in the room without an adult.

In addition to drawing up a programme, it was necessary to collect together the appropriate play material. The toys selected were those which would normally be bought for a child of under 2 years, and as well as 'toys' as we usually think of them, other things such as cotton-reels, Squeezy bottles and scraps of material were collected. These were kept together in the 'treasure box' and were selected to provide a variety of experiences; for example:

visual: emphasis on colour, shape, size (within limits) and surfaces;
tactile: materials with a variety of properties and surfaces;
auditory: different sounds if banged, shaken or rolled.

Much of this material was expendable and needed frequent replacement.

With several of the children, who were most profoundly retarded, the aim was to provide primary sensory experiences; the stimulation in the day room of a ward is limited when compared with that available to a child as he moves around an ordinary house. In other cases it was possible to go on to the use of two elements together and even to some very simple imaginative play.

In putting the programme together, the children's interests and abilities were examined with the aid of a check list covering a range of play materials and the sorts of activities which might be carried out with them. These ranged from sucking and banging to recognizing the toys' specific properties.

Most of the toys were to be made freely available, but a few special toys with parts which might easily be lost or damaged were used only when an adult was close by.

It was intended that the 'play programme' should act as a guide rather than that it should be inflexible, and it was revised from time to time after discussions with the nursing staff.

As well as playing with toys the importance of speech and social activity was also stressed, as can be seen in the following examples taken from the programmes.

Carl: Helping him to walk (5 minutes).
          Simple handling of treasure box material, showing him shaking and banging (5 minutes).
          Speech — talk to him as much as possible while playing with him.
          Repeat any sounds he makes.

Brenda: 10 minutes. (Main activity now throwing. She tends not to occupy herself when she is left alone as well as she used to.) Posting box with small objects as well as more difficult things. 'In and out' play with divided box using small objects as well as bricks. Try to interest her in banging the xylophone. Walking with truck. Try to get her to throw things into a large container. *Speech* – talk to her as much as possible while playing with her. Emphasize the names of things and simple commands. Use these frequently. Do not try to get her to repeat them at this stage, but *do* reinforce by praise and repetition any attempts at words which she does make.

The ideas behind this approach were all discussed at ward meetings and copies of the programmes were displayed in the rooms where the children played. One of the psychologists spent an afternoon on the ward each week so that she could explain and demonstrate their use to new members of staff, but the main task of seeing that the programmes were carried out was the responsibility of the senior nursing staff.

It must be emphasized that it was not possible to carry out this kind of activity if only two staff were on duty. It was found to be easier to put the programmes into practice in the afternoons because the ward was cleaned in the mornings.

Observations suggested that during the experiment three major changes were brought about in the amount of stimulation the children received. Firstly, the adults approached the children more frequently, both to give them toys and to help and encourage them to use them; secondly, the children had access to toys for longer periods of time; thirdly, toys were more varied and more of them gave scope for exploration and experimentation. (Soft toys and many plastic toys can be used only in a limited number of ways.)

As would be expected, some children presented more problems than others. One difficulty faced by the staff was that many of the children made very little social response and any progress was slow. Other difficulties centred around the management of the active ambulant group who settled for a short time only and were often disruptive and destructive. This problem became more pronounced as the children grew bigger and stronger, but we hoped that anything which could be done at an early stage would make it easier to care for them in adult life.

Observations suggested that the lower grade active children were both capable of making a response in a one-to-one situation and able to join in simple group activities if the environment was a relatively formal one.

The problems of these children could not be fully solved in the ward, not least because of the lack of space. They were not considered to be suitable for the kind of activities which were carried on in the school, but still needed to be able to get out of the ward for some part of the day. It would be useful to try a group

121

in a large room with facilities both for physical activities and some simple 'seated' occupations.

At least one of the people supervising such a group should be a man, and initially the project might be set up on an experimental basis. One would not expect the level of attainments of these children to be very high but rather one would hope to reduce the amount of destructive and aggressive behaviour.

Very retarded children formed about two-thirds of the hospital's severely subnormal population. As the provisions in the community improve, this percentage could increase. In some ways this is a parallel to trends in the field of child care as a whole where, to quote Dinnage and Kellmer Pringle (1967), 'as the policy of boarding out is continued and prevention more successful, children in homes will come more and more to consist of a hard core of long stay cases with special problems, emotional, educational and physical'.

RECOMMENDATIONS

A play programme approach should be considered for other wards, particularly those with the younger imbeciles who are not yet ready for school.

With younger brighter children it would be possible to study the emergence of new activities, to look at the order in which manipulative abilities develop and perhaps even to find out something new about how skills are learnt.

Some material would cost nothing to collect, but a sum of money needs to be set aside for additional toys and equipment, perhaps £50 a year for a group such as that in the experimental ward, in addition to the initial outlay on equipment.

The problems of occupying the active, more disruptive children need further consideration.

School Children

The children with mental ages of 18–24 months were a lively active group but, as they lacked security and stability, several of them showed signs of emotional disturbance in addition to their mental and perhaps physical handicaps. The social and emotional sides of their lives were therefore given special attention, the aim being to provide a stable environment in which they felt secure but at the same time could learn about life and gain confidence in themselves. We hoped to provide activities through which they could not only acquire a variety of skills but in which speech and social interaction could be encouraged. We wanted them to become more independent and their lives to become purposeful and happy.

In adult life it was hoped that they would all be able to follow some simple occupation; therefore, increasing their manipulative skills and ability to concentrate was also important. As normal children grow up they become able to persist with, and derive satisfaction from, tasks without being continually under the supervision of adults. It was not clear how far the children could develop this 'inner' control or how far it would be necessary, as a substitute, to teach them to conform to a formal regimen.

PROBLEMS PRESENTED AT SCHOOL

In the experience of the teacher, the children did present many problems when compared with a class of young educationally subnormal children. In such a group the majority of the children are able to occupy themselves fairly happily and constructively as long as an adult is there to give general supervision. The teacher is then able to study and make use of each individual's abilities and interests as well as introducing and organizing specific activities. At first this was not possible in the experimental group because of the noise and temper tantrums, and it took some time for the children and teacher to get to know each other. Initially there did not seem to be a lot of purpose or enjoyment in the children's activities and, because they were unable to use much speech, they were not able to explain their feelings or frustrations to adults. They were destructive and aggressive, their ability to tolerate frustration was low and poor behaviour on the part of one child could easily disrupt the whole group. Most of them enjoyed throwing and kicking, often quite indiscriminately. The fact that some of this behaviour was probably a relic of primitive exploration of the properties of objects rather than 'naughtiness' made it no less real.

To some extent the children's mental age accounted for their behaviour, but their physical size and weight made tantrums a good deal more difficult to manage than they would be with normal 2- to 4-year-olds. Not only was a greater amount of damage done, but it was less easy to control the children physically. Some had difficulties with fine movements which made them very frustrated when they were handling small apparatus. Their gross motor development, however, was often more advanced than their mental age suggested, which meant that their aim was often better and their aggression too well directed.

It is difficult to say to what extent there was an overlay of disturbance caused by organic involvement, but the behaviour of one of the brighter children was certainly very difficult for a day or so before he had a fit.

As a group, the mentally handicapped have a greater number of visual and auditory defects than normals. It is important that these, too, are fully investigated and their implications appreciated by the adults involved in the children's daily care.

Some of these problems will be presented by severely subnormal children living in even the best of home environments, but they were probably emphasized in this group. However, any differences between them and ordinary children should not be allowed to cloud the fact that in many respects retarded children have the same interests as normal ones, learn through the same sorts of experiences and have the same need to be loved and understood by the adults around them.

Children who lack a home-based personal relationship with an adult will always make extra demands for attention and, in addition, several of the children had barely reached a nursery school level and had mental ages of under 3 years. Their teacher recalled such incidents as climbing into the duck pond to retrieve R's shoe which he had thrown there on the way back to the ward and on another occasion wondering where the next pair of trousers were coming from, after he had put his clean pair down the lavatory. Besides needing a lot of help themselves, they disrupted the activities of the older ones. This was not such a problem towards the end, but at first it was very marked. (Tizard described similar outbursts of aggressive behaviour at the beginning of the Brooklands experiment.)

As well as hindering the children's emotional development, their restricted environment gave them relatively little to draw on to form a basis for imaginative activities or conversation. Some of their aggressive behaviour was caused by lack of experience. Although they were eager for new experiences, they had difficulty in accepting them and there were tears and tantrums over who should be first. It was noticed that they responded as if they thought that once their turn was finished they would never have another one.

Looking at the over-all picture, the children's behaviour was in many respects similar to that described by Flint (1968), during the rehabilitation of a group of normal deprived children.

PROBLEMS IN THE WARD

Much of what has been said about the children in school applied equally in the ward; in fact, many of the problems were accentuated because of the additional task of caring for the more retarded. An example of this was the difficulty of setting high standards of behaviour for children who were becoming capable of understanding that they must not throw, when there were a number of children of very limited understanding who were at the throwing stage.

There were children who could not be left for even a short time without supervision and when the staff were occupied with routine tasks, such as bathing and toileting, it was difficult not to treat the whole group *en bloc* (*see* discussion on 'Staffing and ward regimen').

Provisions for the brighter children could not be thought of in total isolation from those which were necessary for the rest of the group.

ORGANIZATION OF THE CLASS

The children attending the hospital school were divided into classes according to age and level of ability, with separate groups for the physically handicapped. Psychological assessments were carried out routinely, annually until the age of 6 years and then at longer intervals depending on their level of functioning.

In most classes there were 12 children and they were looked after by 1 adult who was helped by an older patient. The teacher (assistant supervisor) may or may not have had formal training.

In the experimental ward, all those who were of 'school age' were together in a single class. A qualified teacher with special experience of educationally subnormal children took the group for 3 years from September 1964 to September 1967. Her knowledge of child development was invaluable and she helped to formulate many of the ideas discussed in this section.

The number in the group varied between 10 and 12 at any one time. From December 1965 onwards the principle of having a second adult in the room was established but, prior to this, assistance was intermittent. During the first year it was often a severely subnormal patient who helped and, while it was very useful to have another pair of hands for getting children back to the ward or for toileting, she herself needed a lot of supervision and understanding and often seemed to be as much a responsibility as the children. When the teacher eventually had a full-time helper, she was able to carry out many activities which would not otherwise have been possible. In general, we concluded that while one person can manage a group of older, brighter, severely subnormal children, 2 people are really necessary if the children are young (either mentally or chronologically), immature, or show emotionally disturbed behaviour. All of the school groups contained some of these children and they needed considerable attention if they were to make progress themselves and if they were not to disturb the activities of others. It is not possible to give this kind of attention adequately if the teacher has to deal with a whole group at once. A second person can be very necessary to help with toileting or accidents, and some form of intercom system is essential where any teacher has a class by herself. It is common practice for the teacher to have an assistant, not only in nursery schools, but also in an increasing number of classes in junior training centres.

The relationship between any teacher and helper will vary to some extent according to the temperaments of the people involved, but their roles must always be clearly defined. It is important that the helper should not be asked to do only routine tasks (such as toileting), and that any special skills or interests which she has should be used. She can be very useful in looking after the rest of the class while the teacher is organizing a special activity or perhaps in helping a child who is in a bad mood and in preventing him from disturbing the whole group. The type of person employed as a helper is open to discussion but, particularly with the brighter children, someone who can help to stimulate and teach them is needed.

In the class the teacher had the ultimate responsibility but both her assistants during the second and third years played an active part in teaching the children.

Because the group was such a mixed one, we did find that some tended to disrupt the activities of the others; at times the group was split and half of the children taken to play outside. This policy was adopted partly because there was no direct access to an outside play area. Although the class was sometimes subdivided into two groups of 5, it is not suggested that this would be an ideal size for a class. Children need to be in a large group at times because in a small one opportunities for interaction are restricted.

In some centres it is the practice for children to go to another teacher for activities such as cooking. If the child is immature he may find it difficult to switch from one teacher to another and probably only the older ones could have coped with this for organized activities. All those who enjoyed painting could probably have gone to an 'art' room had there been one. Such a system might be difficult to put into operation' but would provide a chance for them to have extra help with something which they were very keen on, particularly if another member of staff had more to offer in this area than their own teacher. (*N.B.* A scheme similar to this has now been started by the school organizer.)

ORGANIZATION OF THE WARD

Details of staffing and daily routine are given in the section entitled 'Staffing and ward regimen'.

EDUCATIONAL METHODS

The general approach in the classroom was based on 'free play' methods and a wide variety of nursery school activities were introduced. Many of these activities were already being carried out in other classes which were themselves less formal than those in many training centres. In the experimental ward, because there were two adults in the classroom, more activities were available to the children at any one time and it was possible to encourage the children to take more initiative in the selection of play material. The number of occasions when the whole class was expected to join in a single activity, or all to use the same type of equipment under the supervision of the adult, was reduced.

Because we felt that the children were particularly retarded in speech and social development, activities which encouraged them to talk, to play imaginatively and to interact with each other were emphasized in the early stages. Later we tried to strike more of a balance between these and more formal 'work'.

At the beginning it was difficult to know what to talk to the children about, because their experience was very limited and their routine existence provided few events to comment on. During the last year we were able to arrange quite a wide variety of activities and outings, and we felt that the stimulating effects were clearly reflected in the content and quality of the children's speech and play.

If the teacher has a large group of children to look after by herself, she may often have to insist on everyone joining in a single activity. Children at this level have only a limited ability to sustain group interest and, although they may seem to be very obedient, several may be just 'sitting' and getting little or nothing from the activity which is going on. This can be observed in much more mature and stable children than our experimental group.

The time-table was elastic so that it could be suited to the mood and needs of the children at any particular time, but, because we wanted to avoid being entirely without routine, milk-time was relatively formal and during the last year there was a special activity for each day of the week — swimming, tea-shop, fruit, shop (in school) and balloons.

It was found that the period of disturbance lasted for a long time and the situation was made more difficult by the fact that at the beginning of the experiment there was little equipment. Most of the children's energy and emotional tensions had to be contained within the classroom; there was no direct access to an outdoor play area. Gradually, however, they did settle and, as their individual interests emerged, it was possible to help them not only to cope with their tempers more easily, but also to concentrate for longer periods and to interact socially. The adults became skilful in knowing when to intervene and were able to help the children to avoid or overcome their catastrophic reactions to difficulties.

The children did respond to the environment in many ways and were able to find their own level of development through the activities provided for them. Once they had settled down it was easy for a new child coming into the group to find his or her own level. Particularly towards the end, most of them were able to move about in a purposeful and happy manner and it became more possible to arrange the room on nursery school lines with activity-centred areas. Both adults were then able to move around, giving help where it was needed. Although many of the children came to be able to occupy themselves quite well, they always demanded a lot of attention from adults and there was always someone who needed to be encouraged and helped to find something to do.

It is important to note there were signs towards the end of the experiment that the brighter ones were beginning to internalize the values placed on completing tasks, looking after equipment and replacing it in the correct place when it was finished with. Our impression was that, although this was linked with language development, to a large extent it arose from a desire to please the adult with whom they had a close relationship.

The situation might have been eased considerably if it had been possible to build the group up gradually, starting with, say, 4 or 5 of the brighter children.

When we finally reviewed the children's progress we felt that we had not fully solved the problem of meeting the needs of the lower grade group. The methods we attempted to use were not entirely suitable for the children who, for example, remained at the throwing stage throughout the 3 years. It seemed likely that the children in the low grade imbecile/borderline idiot range needed a simpler and more formal environment than the one which we tried to provide. Further research is needed in this area. It may even have been that a little more routine activity would have been useful for all the children.

In the experimental class we had a wider age range in the group than is usual; in the last year it was between 4 and 12 years. Both advantages and disadvantages emerged, but on the whole we felt that, while it is important for children to mix with others older and younger than themselves, it might be better if this did not take place during the whole of their schooling. When some of the older children were away on holiday, it was clear that the younger ones wanted to join in activities from which they were normally excluded. On the other hand, it would have been possible to introduce a freer choice of activities for the older children at an earlier stage if it had not been for the disruptive effect of those who were mentally younger. It was of interest that, when the class was disbanded after the experiment, the children fitted well into their peer groups and several of them were in some ways less difficult to manage.

DAILY LIFE IN THE WARD

The school children spent quite a large part of the day, as well as the week-ends, in the ward and it was in this setting that they did much of their learning about daily living activities. The problem of occupying them in addition to looking after the more handicapped children has already been touched upon, but in spite of these difficulties a wide variety of experiences were introduced. Details of some of these are given in the Appendix and some of the ways in which the problems were tackled are discussed in the section on 'Toys in the ward'.

In general terms, an attempt was made to treat the children as individuals, to provide activities which interested them and to involve them in as many of the adults' tasks as possible. It seemed important that evenings and week-ends were stimulating and enjoyable and that learning and constructive activities were not confined to things which happened in school.

Some rules for behaviour clearly had to be laid down, but the emphasis was on helping the child to keep within them rather than simply dictating to him. Some had a greater need for a disciplined environment than others but it was important that none of them should feel rejected when they had been reprimanded or punished for doing something wrong.

The need to provide a verbally stimulating environment was kept in mind throughout and many of the activities provided both in school and in the ward were geared towards encouraging speech development. When a child has begun to understand and use a system of communication, he can initiate speech activities for himself. Prior to this he is very dependent upon stimulation being provided for him, and in most cases a hospital does not provide naturally the rich environment available to the majority of children living at home.

At a ward meeting it was agreed that we should be consistent in the words used for everyday objects, particularly with children who were just beginning to talk. A list was compiled containing items such as jersey (not jumper, sweater or pullover), beaker (not mug or tumbler).

In addition to providing activities and materials, the adult has an important role to play in helping the children make use of them. This can be done by interpreting the environment verbally and also by creating situations in which the child finds speech a necessary means of communication. For example, the teacher gave information and an explanation of why things should be done: 'You must remember to take them [glasses] back to the ward tonight in case you go home'; 'Yes, you can do those after C has finished' instead of 'not now' or 'later on'. The children were given a choice to make, or asked for information; for example, 'M, would you like to hear a story for a few minutes?'; 'Which one do you want to do?'; 'Did you see Uncle Bert's bike?'.

If talking is to become an interesting and enjoyable activity, the children's own attempts at speech must be rewarded and as far as possible the adult's own comments should be positive and constructive rather than negative. Suggestions can often be made about what the child should do rather than about what he should not. For example, 'Push the pram, not the chair' rather than 'Stop pushing the chair'; 'Not the paper, not J's letter [to wipe up some milk] fetch the cloth'. There is room for explanations here, too. 'You're a very naughtly boy, J; look, now it's broken and the stool won't stand up'.

We received advice about specific problems from the speech therapist but none of the children received regular therapy.

TREATING THE CHILDREN AS INDIVIDUALS — THEIR CLOTHING AND APPEARANCE

An important aspect of our approach was that, throughout the experiment, every attempt was made to treat the children as individuals and help them to develop their own personalities. When large numbers are being looked after together, it is essential to guard against treating them *en bloc*. Individual children were regularly the focus for discussion at ward meetings. It was hoped that these discussions would help the staff to formulate their ideas about each child and would focus attention on his or her special needs.

In addition to adults thinking of children as individuals, children need to be aware of this themselves if they are to understand the behaviour of others and learn to behave in a social way. They need, for example, to have their own clothes and at least a few of their own special possessions. Young children derive a tremendous sense of security from having a favourite toy to carry around with them. Some personal clothing was bought for most of the school children and they all learned to recognize their own clothes. The brighter ones, at least, would be annoyed if they saw someone else wearing their jersey and were particularly possessive about their best 'Sunday' clothes. They enjoyed having something new and liked to come to the adult to be admired.

The question of somewhere to keep individual toys was also considered. In common with other wards, the children had lockers by their beds, but these were easily 'raided' by the younger ones; therefore, bags were made which could be hung up by the children's coats. The children who were really interested in these liked to take them home at week-ends.

A further factor which greatly affected the children's appearance was the way in which their hair was cut. Probably nothing singles out an 'institution' child more than this and yet the nurses found no special problem with ordinary hair styles.

Individual clothing and 'normal' hair greatly improved the children's appearance. The importance of this cannot be over-emphasized when considering whether or not they would be found acceptable by members of the public. They were in contact with them, perhaps more than one might think.

CO-OPERATION BETWEEN THE WARD AND SCHOOL

An important feature of this study was the extent of co-operation between the ward and the school. Both teachers and nursing staff found this to be very valuable and there was a considerable overlap in the activities they carried out with the children. Examples of this are to be found in the topics discussed in the Appendix. Wherever there is close co-operation, teaching can become a more continuous process and the children can be handled more consistently and according to their individual needs.

In addition to any long-term effects upon the children, the adults found that more contact with each other made day-to-day problems easier to handle, to the advantage of everyone concerned.

The student nurses spent some time in the school as part of their training. During this period they had a real opportunity to participate in the class activities and to learn the purpose behind them. This provided a good basis for mutual understanding in the future. It would seem equally important that teachers have experience of the work of nurses or 'houseparents'.

RECOMMENDATIONS

In the school

The classes in school should not exceed the size recommended by the Scott Committee, that is, 1 teacher to 10 children (Ministry of Health, 1961). If the children are mentally very young, or show disturbed behaviour, the teacher should have a regular helper.

An intercom system is essential where any teacher has a class by herself, and is highly desirable even if this is not the case.

Education and training in school are carried out more easily if the children are grouped mainly according to age and ability rather than each class containing a cross-section. This system, already used in the hospital school, is therefore recommended. It is an important feature that the groupings are flexible enough to allow the needs of individual children to be met.

Further consideration should be given to the problem of teaching the children functioning towards the bottom of the imbecile range. These represented over 10 per cent of our school population. Their problems may well overlap with those of a number of active children who are considered too low grade to be suitable for a training centre.

In the ward

A number of suggestions have been put forward in the sections on 'Staffing and ward regimen' and 'Toys in the ward'.

The question of the care of active lower grade children should be considered in relation to the ward as well as the school. It is this group which presented the greatest problem with regard to management.

Contact between the ward and school

The close contact achieved between ward and school was found to be very valuable, and it is recommended that ways of increasing this contact generally should be discussed.

Personal possessions

Personal clothing should be provided for the trainable imbecile in particular and this should resemble that worn by normal children.

Those who show an interest in toys should have somewhere to keep personal possessions.

More attention should be paid to the way in which hair is cut; this could be an important factor in improving appearance and social acceptability.

Staff training

As the problems presented by the children were examined in detail it became clear that they could not be treated as an isolated group. They were severely subnormal, but their needs overlapped with those of ordinary children in residential care and with those of the maladjusted and disturbed.

It seems to us, and to other workers in the field of child care, that the stage has been reached when we should bridge the gap between the divisions which have developed historically. It is time to take a fresh look at the training of staff. Opportunities to work with both normal and handicapped children would be valuable, whatever field is being specialized in.

Toys in the Ward

Because children learn through exploration and through play, it is important that their environment be an interesting and stimulating one. The need for toys is of extra importance in hospital because a ward can be very bare when compared with an ordinary home and therefore there are limited opportunities for 'incidental' learning to take place.

The toys selected for a ward should be as varied as possible within the limit of the mental level of the children and, of necessity, hard wearing if they are to last. However, there is also a need for a large and continuing supply of easily replaceable toys and objects.

The children tended to fall into three groups and the toys also will be discussed in this way. In the first group were the 6 most retarded children, with mental ages of 1 year or under and chronological ages (in the last year) of 7 years and over. This group enjoyed rattles, squeaky toys, balls and the Turnabout (designed as a rocking boat or push-car). They also enjoyed strings of 'jangly' toys which the staff made for them and the 'treasure box' which is described in relation to the play programme.

The second group consisted of 3 or 4 slightly brighter and more active children and, for part of the time, the younger bright ones. They all enjoyed constructional toys, the blackboard and chalks, dressing-up clothes and books. In their play they showed considerable overlap with the groups above and below them. Inasmuch as they were starting to copy the other children and adults, they needed dolls and prams; trucks were particularly useful as they could be used in such a variety of ways. Cuddly toys were used only occasionally.

The brightest children enjoyed a wide variety of toys, ranging from dolls, books and scissors to simple puzzles. The puzzles and other 'sets' of materials for this group were kept in the cupboard in the ward office. They were looked after very carefully and lasted well. An indoor climbing frame and slide and a trampoline were also a great success. The majority of the active children enjoyed using the trampoline, particularly when it was not possible for them to go out into the playground. It was found that only a minimum of supervision was necessary and there were no accidents during the year in which it was in use.

The Turnabout and dressing-up clothes were always a useful standby and we found that soft knitted balls helped to direct indoor throwing into a safe and acceptable channel. (These are quick and easy to make and might be provided by parents and friends.)

The activities in which the children were interested varied from time to time and any piece of equipment lost its fascination after a while. For this reason toys should be changed fairly frequently; that is, new ones should be introduced and those which the children appear not to be using very much should be put away and brought out again at a later date.

Providing adequate stimulation does not stop with buying toys. Extra equipment needs extra cupboard space if it is to be looked after properly, and having toys available does mean extra work for the adult. Not only is it important that the toys should be out for as much of the day as possible, but they must be put away and checked carefully each time. An eight-piece puzzle with only six or seven pieces has lost all of its usefulness. A few of the brighter children may be able to accept quite a lot of responsibility for caring for toys, but essentially the adults must make it part of their daily routine. It is a considerable advantage if the staff know the children well because they will know how they are likely to behave, who needs close supervision and when. It must be realized that it takes time for the adult to learn both to set a high standard of care for the toys and to make the best use of them with any particular group. Storage always remained something of a problem because although we were able to use the small cubicle in the ward, this meant that it was out of action for anything else. Ideally, a number of fitted cupboards are needed, keeping in mind that trucks, cots and rockers take up a lot of room.

Some losses of equipment are bound to occur at times and so, too, are breakages. Although the toys were selected carefully, those suitable for the children's mental level were not always suitable for their strength. Some toys were specially made within the hospital and these and the Turnabout lasted longer than most others. Toys sent for repair took a long time to come back but it is likely that major repairs or 'writing off' could have been delayed if minor repairs had been carried out quickly. It would be very useful for both the school and the ward if one person were responsible for repairs, wherever possible carrying them out on the spot. Some equipment would last much longer if it were reinforced before being used.

Besides toys to play with, somewhere to play is important. While the more handicapped children needed a lot of help and encouragement to use toys, the older ones played with relatively little supervision provided they had somewhere to do so. If they were to occupy themselves happily, they had to be free from interruptions from those who could not settle down. Sister's office was used a good deal for this purpose although it was not always convenient. A third room would have been useful. The office was also used for special activities such as cutting out or painting.

A good deal of skill and work is involved if full use is to be made of toys in the ward. It is not easy to teach staff to take proper care of play material and it is important that high standards are set by those responsible for training. Everything we know about child development indicates that it is essential that this be done if children are to be helped to make the best use of their abilities.

RECOMMENDATIONS

(1)   There should be provision for a good supply of toys in all wards and adequate cupboard space in which to keep them.

(2)   A high standard of care for play material should be maintained.

(3)   There should be some equipment set aside for any brighter children who can occupy themselves with a minimum of supervision.

(4)   There should be somewhere for them to play without being disturbed by the others.

(5)   There should be someone whose special responsibility it is to repair and reinforce toys and other equipment, and it is suggested that as much of this as is possible should be done on the spot.

The Adventure Playground

In common with all young children, the experimental group had a great deal of energy to expend and a need to climb and swing and run to find out what they could do with their bodies and to increase their control over them.

There was relatively little room in the ward for 20 children, of whom at least 13 were very active. The best use possible was made of the space available, but it was felt that an outdoor playground was the real solution. There was a hard court shared with the ward next door, but there was nothing to play with except for bicycles and trucks and no good opportunity for working off surplus energy or enjoying physical movement. The children were mentally too young to understand team games and needed opportunities to express themselves as individuals and follow up their own interests.

We had about quarter of an acre of rough grass adjacent to the ward which we were able to make into an adventure playground.

Before planning the playground we decided to look at current provisions for normal children. Both physical size and mental ability had to be taken into account. We received advice from the Play Leadership Organiser for the Greater London Council and talked to the Supervisor for Under Fives in the GLC Parks

Department and the Area Supervisor for Play Parks, who came to help to construct some of the apparatus.

APPARATUS

The apparatus eventually chosen provided opportunities for exercising a variety of skills. Gross motor activities were catered for, but we also had equipment which we hoped would provide a direct stimulus to imaginative play. A description of the apparatus in the playground follows.

Grass mound

There was a grass mound, roughly 1.8 m high and 7.2 m in diameter (6 X 24 feet). The Play Leadership Organiser recommended that it should be sown with rye grass, which is particularly suitable as the roots grip the soil and prevent its movement.

Slide

A slide was erected against the grass mound. We used an end section of a Fibreglass escape chute 750 mm (2 feet 6 inches) in diameter. A wooden one could have been made and would have required a plank 3 m X 375 mm X 75 mm (10 feet X 15 inches X 3 inches) and linoleum of good quality of approximately the same size.

Climbing net

A climbing net was hung over a central support and fixed to the ground at both ends; its height was about 1.8 m (6 feet). We were fortunate in that both the net and rope ladder were made in Terylene for us at a Royal Naval Training School, but climbing nets can be obtained from educational suppliers.

Log-climbing pile

This piece of climbing apparatus was made from logs and planks. Viewed from the side it was triangular in shape with a base of about 3.6 m (12 feet) and rising to about 1.8 m (6 feet) in the centre.

Cat-walk

The cat-walk consisted of a series of planks to walk along which were raised above the ground and sloping at a variety of angles. The highest ends, which were not more than about 900 mm (3 feet) above the ground, were reached by a short ladder with four steps.

135

Swing

We already had a set of three swings, but we were advised that conventional swings could be dangerous even for normal children and the substitution of hanging motor tyres and a slat 'ladder' was suggested. The rings fixing the tyres to the original chains could be attached by placing a broad iron band inside the tyre and securing it with double bolts. The tyres were a gift from a local garage. We did keep one swing with a bucket seat, however, because we felt that this would be specially useful for the more severely handicapped children.

Ropes

Ropes were slung across the branches of a tree so that the children could sit in the loop. The ropes were near the grass mound so that they could climb up and swing themselves down. These cost only a few pounds and were very popular.

Barrels

Barrels were set in a simple frame to prevent them being rolled. They need to be painted to prevent them from deteriorating. Barrels are much safer than large concrete pipes, as children tend to misjudge the height and may bang their heads.

Sand pit

If the group of children using the playground is fairly large, two small sand pits rather than one large one will make for greater tranquillity. We did not have sufficient space for this.

Our sand pit was sunk into the ground and concrete lined. However, a much simpler, cheaper structure was recommended to us as follows: four elm boards bolted together making a sand pit measuring 3 m (10 feet) square. If this can be set on a slight incline the drainage will look after itself.

Specifications

Sand pit: 4 elm boards 3 m × 450 mm × 18 mm (10 feet × 18 inches × ¾ inch). Corners to be strengthened with 8 angle-irons.
Sand: Washed river sand which is not too sharp.
This type of sand pit has been found to be very successful by the GLC Parks Department.

Playhouse

The playhouse was a very simple design and was made to our specifications (on a voluntary basis) by the workers at a firm of car manufacturers. It was 2.1 m square and 1.5 m high (7 X 7 X 5 feet) and had a swing door with no handle or lock and a window (without glass) 300 mm (1 foot) square in one wall. A sloping roof is preferable. The playhouse was set on a concrete base and this proved to be expensive.

Steering wheel

A steering wheel was attached to a piece of metal tubing and fixed into the ground; nearby was something for the children to sit on so that they could 'drive'.

Seats

These were made with timber and seat brackets.

We were very fortunate in having a gift of money to build the playground and, in addition, much of the equipment was donated or made for us. The playground has certainly proved to be popular with the active children, whatever their level of ability, and the nursing staff, too, have found it a valuable addition to the ward. Skill in swinging, balancing and climbing has improved and now it is only the more handicapped who need help; at first everyone needed quite a lot of assistance. Sometimes they needed the adults to show them what to do, such as on the climbing net; sometimes they learned from others, for example, one boy learned to swing on the ropes and the others copied him. Although the children were still at the level of requiring considerable supervision, 4 of them could be allowed out alone for a short time and 1 of the more handicapped could go out alone when the others were at school. The playground had a special value for a very over-active girl who was a great problem to manage indoors.

There were no serious accidents during the 18 months that the playground was in use and it was only the swings which seemed to be potentially dangerous. We did substitute a tyre and a ladder for two of them, but the remaining swing was the most popular. We feel that at least one swing should be kept, although it will be necessary to chain it up at times. The danger is of another child being hurt rather than the child who is swinging.

Some of the children had their favourite pieces of apparatus but on the whole they did move around, using most of the things in turn. They enjoyed all the equipment for climbing and swinging but did not make so much use of the barrels or the chute. This may have been because the slope on the latter was a relatively short one and they had to pull themselves down it and could not slide properly. It is likely that children capable of more co-operative and imaginative play would have used the chute and barrels more often.

Nearly everyone made use of the sand pit but the younger ones needed some

137

help. The management of sand can be a problem as the children did tend to throw and it might not be suitable for all wards. It is important that the sand be kept damp enough for building (*see* notes on 'Sand' in the Appendix).

There was not very much room for tricycles, trucks and prams to be used in the playground and these were kept mainly on the hard court. In planning another playground a special area might be set aside for this. A clear space on the grass is needed for the very handicapped children to sit and where the paddling pool can be taken in the fine weather.

We did not see very much real group activity in the playground and the children tended to go off on their own. They did not seem to be at the stage of spontaneously playing games, such as 'follow my leader'. Sometimes one child did organize a group in the Wendy house or behind the grass mound. 'Private' places such as this are probably particularly important for children living together in large numbers.

We did not have direct access to the playground, although this would have made the task of supervision by the staff much easier, particularly if only two nurses were on duty. Ideally, 'access' should be combined with somewhere for shoes to be changed. The nurses found that it was difficult to use the playground if it was wet or cold as the children could get very muddy and might come in saying that they were cold. To enable the play area to be used as fully as possible, it was suggested that we had a 'hard standing' made from concrete paving slabs 600 mm (2 feet) square around each piece of apparatus. This is important with blind children as the change of surface underfoot tells them that they are approaching an obstacle.

It is important that a toilet should be readily accessible from the playground.

RECOMMENDATIONS

An adventure playground would be useful for all wards with active children, although the design might be varied to meet individual needs.

Visitors

The general policy throughout the hospital was to encourage visiting, and wherever possible we tried to maintain or re-establish contact with the children's homes. Certainly a large number enjoyed being visited and were pleased to have the undivided attention of their own special adult whom they learned to rely on. Besides any emotional gains, the visitors brought many new experiences to the child and helped him to become familiar with and understand more of the outside world.

Several of the children's parents did visit them regularly, taking them out or home for week-ends or for holidays. However, in spite of the efforts of the social workers, some children had no visitors and we realized that for some parents it was difficult and painful to accept the presence of their child. In addition, there were those with no relatives, or at least none living nearby. For these groups 'aunties' seemed to be the answer, although we took care always to keep the parents informed about what was going on. We were very fortunate in recruiting several aunties for the children who, for one reason or another, were not visited regularly. These were mostly married women whose families were either grown up or at least were at school. One auntie was introduced to us by a friend who was working in the medical records department at the time and she in turn introduced others. These five or six aunties, who visited regularly, all knew each other through the local church. Those visiting the lower grade children chiefly took them for walks or out to play with a ball, while those visiting the brighter ones took them to the tea-shop or outside the hospital. There was sometimes a problem of where to go if the weather was bad, but the opening of a Friends' Centre went some way towards overcoming this problem. If there had been an extra room in the ward this would have been one use for it, particularly in the winter. We made a point of an auntie taking out only the child she had come to visit so that he knew that she was specially for him, but aunties did sometimes accompany the group on outings or trips to the pool where they provided a very valuable extra pair of hands.

During the last year, 5 children were visited by their parents at least once a fortnight and 3 more at least once a month. The remainder were visited less frequently and 7 had contact with their families only once a year or less. Also during the final year, 5 children had aunties who came to see them at least once a fortnight and 3 were visited about once a month. In all, 15 of the 20 children had regular contact (at least once a month) with their families or an auntie.

Four of the aunties visited for more than 2 years, and asking voluntary workers to take an interest in one particular child seemed to be a good way of making use of their help. One or two aunties were anxious to give further assistance to the teachers or nursing staff and their help was gladly accepted. Throughout, the ward staff and teachers played a very important role in making the parents and other visitors feel welcome and in encouraging them to come as often as possible. The general training and experience given to the children helped by making them more socially acceptable, and improved clothing and haircuts must surely have had a similar effect.

Another group of people who played a part in the ward were the girls from a local grammar school who came during the week (Monday to Friday) to play with the children. They were chiefly sixth formers but in the summer term there were also fifth form girls who would be coming the following year.

About 30 girls were on the rota at any one time and 2 or 3 came each evening between 5.30 and 6.30 p.m. In the warm light evenings they went out of doors into the adventure playground, but more often they took 3 or 4 children into Sister's office and used toys from the cupboard. At first it was usually the brighter, more co-operative children who went; then all the full-time school children took it in turn, although the younger ones joined in for only short periods and did not stay for the whole session.

These arrangements did not cause much extra work because the ward routine was already fairly flexible. There was usually some clearing up to do afterwards, but this was relatively little compared with the pleasure the children derived from their visitors. They looked forward to their coming and really enjoyed the time spent with them.

We did realize that we would be increasing the number of people the children had to deal with but, on the other hand, their roles would be fairly clear, confined to a certain part of the day and certain kinds of activities. The children who could talk referred to them as 'the girls' and appeared to be able to group them together.

The fact that the girls visited regularly from March 1966 suggests that they, too, derived a good deal from the visits. Before the first group came a member of the psychology department gave an introductory talk at the school and this was followed by a further talk at the end of each school year. When the first group arrived, one of the psychologists met them on the ward to help them over their initial visit. Subsequently, 'new' girls came with people who had already been visiting for some time. The girls were always treated as responsible people making a useful contribution, but it was always emphasized that they could turn to the nursing staff for support whenever they needed it. Both the attitude of the nurses and the continued liaison with the school were important factors in the success of the scheme.

The school girls were, on the whole, discouraged from visiting and taking out individual children on a regular basis because we felt that there should at least be a chance for any such relationship to continue over a number of years. Many of the girls would be leaving the area to go on to further training in a year or two's time. Most of the aunties were married women who were relatively settled.

Our experiences support the view that voluntary helpers with no special training can make a valuable contribution to the care of the children. However, it is important that there be close liaison between them and the trained staff, in particular when they first begin to visit.

RECOMMENDATIONS

(1)   Parents should be encouraged to visit their children whenever possible and aunties should be sought for children who have no regular visitors.

(2)   Encouragement should be given to school children wanting to come to play with the children. Care should be taken to organize their initial visits and to provide continued support. The nursing staff have a major role to play in this respect.

Parents' Meetings

INVOLVEMENT OF PARENTS AND VOLUNTARY WORKERS

Parents' meetings were held three or four times a year in order to involve the parents in the experiment. The aunties or voluntary workers were also invited. These meetings were attended by all the staff who attended the weekly meetings and, in addition, by Professor Tizard and Mrs. Goldschmied, who helped us greatly throughout the experiment. Often the heads of departments involved attended. These meetings were run on the same lines as the weekly meetings and the parents were asked for their comments. We gave yearly reports on the progress of individual children. It is difficult to say whether the parents of the children in the experimental ward showed more interest than the parents of children from other wards because it is not something we can measure at present. One criterion for the success of the meetings was that the parents themselves voted to continue them when the experiment ended.

The parents were also involved in other ways. They were encouraged to visit their children and to have them home as much as possible. The parents provided a shed in which to keep outdoor toys. They helped at Christmas parties and at least three parents helped on outings or in the swimming pool. The aunties also helped in this way. One auntie gave us a generous gift of money which was used to equip the adventure playground and to provide extra toys for the class. It was useful to have a sum of money on which one could draw at short notice.

SAMPLE OF PARENTS' MEETINGS

Sunday, 6th March, 1966
Present: 9 members of staff, 11 parents and 4 aunties.
Apologies for absence etc.

Professor Tizard opened the meeting. He said that the ward had now been running for two years; therefore, we wanted to review the progress we had made and discuss the plans for next year.

141

A father offered to dismantle a Jungle Gym we had been given by the Spastics Society and transport it to the ward.

The altered date for the ITV film was reported.

Progress report from staff

A detailed report of the progress of all the children in daily living skills was given.

In January, 1966, 19 of the 20 children in the ward showed some improvement in these skills; 14 of the children were more advanced in daily living skills than their mental age; in 6 children their daily living skills were equal to their mental age.

Seven of the children showed more improvement than their controls; 10 showed roughly the same improvement as the controls and 3 showed less improvement. This is a crude breakdown of the results but it is proposed to work them out in more detail when the experiment is concluded next year.

A detailed report on speech and social behaviour followed. M, J, T, and S are the four children who speak most and they have all increased their vocabulary and are now using more complex sentences. C, S, N and J use fewer words but they have also increased their vocabularies and spend a lot of time practising the new words they learn. K did not talk when we started the experiment but he is now using single words and is much more interested in what is going on. The latter is true of all the school children, and those who had difficulties in joining in with the others are improving in this respect.

M, E and C all attend school part-time. None of them spoke when the experiment started, but now C is using single words and the others are making a much wider variety of sounds than they did before.

The children who do not attend school are mentally the youngest and we would not expect to see quite so much progress in this group. None of them really speaks — several make very little contact with people or objects. We have seen some small changes, however, and hope that as the play programme which is being carried out in the ward is continued, the number of these will increase.

The teacher reported on improvements noticed in the school children:

(1)   the children's vocabulary has increased;
(2)   they gather around with interest when something new is introduced instead of immediately rejecting it;
(3)   most of the children have a longer span of concentration;
(4)   they enjoy songs and movement to music;
(5)   1 or 2 children are just beginning to accept and understand why they are being disciplined, instead of having a temper tantrum when corrected;
(6)   there is no longer a set time for taking the children to the toilet;

(7)   the children all get on better together as a group. This was
      particularly noticeable at the Christmas party.

Sister thanked the parents for the Turnabout they had given the children
and for the climbing frame from a women's club.

Charge nurse said he had noticed that the children had improved since
he had been on the ward.

A mother offered an old motor-bicycle for the adventure playground.
One of the psychologists said that she would consult the other people
concerned in planning the playground about this. Some of the parents
expressed anxiety about the continuation of the ward after next year. They
were assured that the children would remain in the same ward for the time
being and, it was hoped, as long as they stayed in the hospital.

Professor Tizard was asked whether it helped our handicapped children
to mix with normal children. There was some discussion on this. It was
agreed that mentally handicapped children were quite accepted at home
by their own brothers and sisters. However, mixing our children with
normal children who are not in their own family must be done carefully
and for short periods at a time. A mother thought that normal children
should be told that our children were different and then she said that for
short periods they were very happy to play with them. One or two of the
parents mentioned how upset they had been when they first visited the
large wards at another hospital. On the whole it was felt that children
accepted mentally handicapped children more easily than adults but, again,
it required care to mix normal and subnormal children.

Professor Tizard talked about the future of the children and pointed
out that we must accept that they would not be formally educable. However,
some of them would be able to lead quite a full life in a sheltered environment when they were grown up — perhaps work in a sheltered workshop
and be socially independent. We believe that learning through play when
they are children will help the severely subnormal to develop so that they
can live as full an adult life as possible in a sheltered environment.

One of the parents asked Professor Tizard when the children's ability
stopped developing; he said probably at about 16 years when the actual
level of intelligence, in the sense of problem solving, ceased to develop.
However, the use they could make of their intelligence continued to
increase with experience, and therefore social development and personal
skills also go on increasing during the teens and twenties.

DISCUSSION AND RECOMMENDATIONS

Parents' meetings at ward level are one means of involving the parents in the
care of their children. It also seems useful to have combined meetings of

parents and 'aunties' and 'uncles'. As Professor Tizard said at a recent meeting — the success of residential institutions in the future may depend largely upon the extent to which they can make use of voluntary help. He also pointed out, in relation to the place of parents in the lives of children in residential care, that they were the constant figures in the children's lives.

It might be difficult to have these meetings for every ward in the hospital, but perhaps two wards could have combined meetings two or three times a year.

We believe that parents' meetings for all the psychiatric wards would be too big and, therefore, impersonal. The parents were always particularly interested in the progress of their own child and it was out of this that their wider interests often developed (that is, in the mentally handicapped as a whole and the children in the ward and hospital in particular). Parents' meetings are the most effective way of involving the parents in some way in the running of the ward and of fostering the links between the home and the hospital.

The Attainments of the Experimental Children and of a Control Group

Throughout the study of a series of measures was made in order to be able to compare the progress of the experimental children with that of a control group.

FORMAL TESTS RESULTS — MEASURES OF VERBAL AND NON-VERBAL ABILITY

The method of selecting the children and the representativeness of the sample have already been described. Initially only 5 pairs out of the total of 20 could be assessed on a formal intelligence test, in this case the Minnesota Pre-School Scale (this was chosen because it provides measures of verbal and non-verbal ability separately). The children were all below the level of the scale which does not go below IQ 49 and mental ages had to be estimated by looking at the chronological age at which an average child (that is, one with IQ 100) obtains any given score. The non-verbal scale starts at 2½ years and the verbal at 18 months. A child of 2½ years must pass three items on the non-verbal scale to obtain an IQ of 100. For the purposes of matching children not reaching this standard, those scoring on one item were credited with a mental age of 2 years, and on two items with a mental age of 2 years 3 months.

The children below this level could not be assessed on a scale of infant development because of their lack of responsiveness both to adults and to their surroundings in general. Instead, their behaviour was classified in terms of Piaget's sensorimotor stages following the method described by Woodward (1963) for studying severely handicapped children. The sensorimotor period lasts from birth to about 18—24 months, and Piaget describes six major substages. From observations of his own children he suggests the following approximate age ranges: stage III, 4—8 months; stage IV, 8—12 months; stage V, 12—18 months; stage VI, 18 months and above.

In order to be able to look at the children's attainments in relation to their chronological ages, it was decided to ascribe a single mental age to each stage. Although these represent only rough approximations, they seem useful for present purposes. It should be borne in mind that in most cases the children's mental ages were below one-fifth of their chronological ages and variations of several months of mental age would make no real difference to an IQ score. The ages adopted were as follows.

Piaget stage	Age
III	6 months
IV	9 months
V	12 months
VI	18 months

Speech was assessed on an *ad hoc* scale using norms from existing developmental scales.

Speech scale	Age
Two different syllables	3 months
Two-syllable babble	6 months
One or two clear words	9 months
Three clear words	12 months
Four or five clear words	15 months

The original status of the experimental and control groups is given in Table 4.1. The information is given in terms of mental ages, as this gives a clearer picture of the level of behaviour under discussion.

The higher and lower grade children are discussed separately.

The imbecile group (pairs 1—9)

Table 4.2 gives a summary of the status of the children in 1964 and Table 4.3 of their status in 1967. Table 4.4 summarizes the amount of change over the 3 years.

TABLE 4.1

The 20 Matched Pairs Selected for Study in 1964

Pair	Experimental group				Controls			
	Age	Mental age		Non-verbal quotient	Age	Mental age		Non-verbal quotient
		Non-verbal	Verbal			Non-verbal	Verbal	
1M	9y 2m	3y 7m	2y 7m	39	8y 6m	2y 10m	2y 10m	33
2	7y 5m	2y 7m	2y 10m	35	6y 2m	2y 2m	1y 7m	35
3M	6y 11m	2y 4m	2y 1m	34	6y 11m	2y 2m	2y 3m	31
4M	5y 10m	2y	1y 8m	34	5y 8m	2y 7m	2y 4m	46
5	9y 1m	2y	2y	22	8y 7m	2y	1y 6m	23
6M	1y 5m	6m	6m	35	1y 5m	6m	3m	35
7M	6y 10m	1y 6m	6m	22	6y 10m	1y 6m	9m	22
8M	3y 8m	1y	6m	27	4y 2m	1y	6m	24
9	3y 11m	1y	3m	26	3y 5m	1y	3m	29
10	5y 4m	1y 6m	1y 3m	28	7y 2m	1y 6m	1y 3m	19
11	5y 1m	1y	0	20	5y	1y	3m	20
12M	7y 7m	1y 6m	6m	20	7y 6m	1y 6m	3m	20
13	5y 3m	1y	6m	19	5y 6m	1y	6m	18
14	4y 2m	9m	3m	18	5y	1y	6m	20
15M	5y 10m	1y	0	17	5y 11m	1y	3m	17
16	9y 2m	1y 6m	3m	16	9y 3m	1y 6m	6m	16
17	6y 2m	9m	0	12	6y 6m	1y	3m	15
18	6y 3m	9m	0	12	6y 1m	9m	0	12
19	7y	9m	3m	11	7y 6m	9m	0	10
20	7y 6m	9m	0	10	8y 1m	1y	6m	12

Pairs 1 – 5 assessed on the Minnesota Pre-School Scale

M = Mongol

TABLE 4.2

Status of the Imbecile Children in 1964

| | Chronological age | | Mental age – verbal | | Mental age – non-verbal | |
	Mean	Range	Mean	Range	Mean	Range
Experimental group	6y 0m	1y 5m–9y 2m	1y 5m	3m–2y 10m	1y 10m	6m–3y 7m
Control group	5y 9m	1y 5m–8y 7m	1y 4m	3m–2y 10m	1y 9m	6m–2y 10m

TABLE 4.3

Status of the Imbecile Children in 1967

| | Mental age – verbal | | Mental age – non-verbal | |
	Mean	Range	Mean	Range
Experimental group	2y 10m	1y 7m–5y 1m	3y 8m	2y 4m–5y 0m
Control group	2y 0m	3m–3y 10m	2y 7m	1y 6m–4y 6m

TABLE 4.4

Progress Made by the Imbecile Children over the Period of the Experiment

| | Mental age – verbal | | Mental age – non-verbal | |
	Mean	Range	Mean	Range
Experimental group	1y 5m	8m–2y 5m	1y 10m	10m–2y 11m
Control group	8m	None–1y 5m	10m	None–1y 8m

(In view of the children's intelligence, about 3–4 months' progress in non-verbal tests would be expected annually.)

Originally the means and range of scores for the two groups were very close. One girl in the experimental group (pair 1) did have a non-verbal mental age of 9 months higher than anyone else, but in fact she made less progress than her control. The boy in the control group (pair 9) who made no progress verbally, remaining with a mental age of 3 months throughout, did not by himself account for the low mean score. The data were treated statistically using a simplification of Students' t (Sandler, 1955). This test was used for all differences (Tables 4.1–4.4) except when specified. The differences between the amount of progress made by the two groups in verbal ability was significant at the .05 level and in non-verbal ability at the .01 level, both differences being in favour of the experimental group.

These results differ from those obtained in the Brooklands study, where the experimental group showed a significant gain in verbal scores but not in non-verbal areas.

Figure 4.1 compares the pattern found by Tizard with that of the present study. It can be seen that in our groups the initial means for the verbal and non-verbal mental ages were much closer together than at Brooklands. There were children in both the experimental and the control groups with verbal ability equal to, or higher than, non-verbal ability.

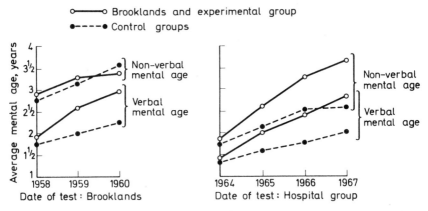

Figure 4.1. Intelligence test results for Brooklands and control groups and for the present hospital experimental and control groups

It seemed to us that a number of factors in the children's environment might be expected to improve their non-verbal skills. A good deal of thought had been given to trying to introduce a wider variety of experience and of stimulating their interest in using their hands. Because many of the 'school' activities were also carried out in the ward, the children spent more time in a learning situation. Emphasis was also placed on helping the children to deal with frustration so that they were able to persist with, and learn from, tasks which they would other- wise have abandoned. Any increases in attention span resulting from their becoming more settled emotionally could also contribute.

While these factors also applied at Brooklands, it may have been that they had a greater effect in our ward because the children were initially mentally younger and more immature. The average non-verbal quotient on entry to Brooklands was nearly 40, compared with 30 for our group. The average non-verbal mental age was 2 years 10 months, compared with 1 year 10 months.

Although the Brooklands children were not selected according to their degree of emotional disturbance, 2 were returned to the main hospital because of severe behaviour disorders. All our group were retained regardless of their behaviour.

It was both helpful and interesting to us that Miss Jeffree, who was doing research with young handicapped children with Mr. Cashdan in the Department of Education at Manchester, came to the hospital to administer a battery of 'experience' tests to some of the brighter groups. She assessed the children's experience of 'everyday life', 'outings and occasions' and 'adult activities' and has very kindly allowed her results to be quoted. The 3 children tested from the experimental ward had a mean score in each area higher than that of the other hospital groups (including a group of girls who were living in a hostel for older girls and women outside the hospital). The difference could not be explained purely in terms of mental age.

The lower grade group (pairs 10–20)

Tables 4.5 and 4.6 give summaries of the children's status in 1964 and in 1967. Table 4.7 summarizes the amount of change over the 3 years.

TABLE 4.5

Status of the Lower Grade Children in 1964

	Chronological age		Mental age – verbal		Mental age – non-verbal	
	Mean	Range	Mean	Range	Mean	Range
Experimental group	6y 4m	4y 2m–9y 2m	3m	0m–15m	12m	9m–18m
Control	6y 8m	5y 0m–9y 3m	5m	0m–15m	13m	9m–18m

There was a slight tendency for the experimental group to do better than their controls, but t-tests showed no significant difference on either verbal or non-verbal measures ($p > .10$ in both cases). The most striking factor was the very limited amount of change which took place. Several children did not make any progress or seemed to do less at the end of the 3 years than they did at the beginning. As this is such an important feature of children functioning at this

149

TABLE 4.6

Status of the Lower Grade Children in 1967

	Mental age – verbal		Mental age – non-verbal	
	Mean	Range	Mean	Range
Experimental group	5m	0m–19m	14m	6m–26m
Control group	4m	0m–15m	13m	6m–18m

TABLE 4.7

Progress Made by the Lower Grade Children over the Period of the Experiment

	Mental age – verbal		Mental age – non-verbal	
	Mean	Range	Mean	Range
Experimental group	2m	–3m – +13m	2m	–3m – +8m
Control group	–1m	–6m – +3m	–1m	–6m – +3m

level, Table 4.8 gives the direction of the changes which were observed. The differences between the experimental group and the control group are not statistically significant ($p > .10$).

TABLE 4.8

	Positive	No change	Negative
Experimental group	8	10	4
Control group	3	13	6

LANGUAGE AND SOCIAL RESPONSES

In the Brooklands study, assessments of the changes in the children's social and emotional status were qualitative as there were no suitable ready-made scales or tests of personality and there was no time to construct suitable *ad hoc* measures. In many ways we found ourselves in a similar position, particularly as we were doing the work in addition to ordinary clinical duties. However, during the course of the project a paper was published by Hulme and Lunzer (1966) which drew our attention to a most useful quantitative method of analysing the level of the children's play, and we were able to make use of this.

A number of *ad hoc* scales were put together for use with the more severely retarded, lower grade children. In order to increase the reliability of the observations, information was collected from more than one source whenever this was possible.

Because it was necessary to use different methods to assess children functioning at different levels, the imbecile and lower grade groups are again discussed separately.

The imbecile group

Many of our objectives for the children depended on increasing their ability to communicate. For this reason, and because changes in emotional adjustment can be expected to be reflected in speech development, language was chosen for further study. The children's mental ages fell largely within the 18 months to 4 years range which Piaget has described as the preconceptual stage, during which we see the appearance of symbolic functioning. Since the learning of verbal labels is a long process, the child must invent symbols for his needs, and symbolic activity can be observed not only in the systematic acquisition of language, but also in imaginative play (Piaget, 1962). Both of these areas were studied by carrying out detailed observations during the children's day-to-day activities. During the final year the 7 pairs of children who were attending school full-time were compared. Each child was observed in the classroom for a total of twelve 10-minute periods and his behaviour scored in the following ways.

(1)   Number of words used — the total number of words used, with the exception of those spoken during any repetitive speech work carried out with the teacher.

(2)   Number of different words used (with the exception described above).

(3)   Complexity of sentence structure. This was measured on a scale devised during a pilot study in which scores were given according to the number of components in a sentence and whether nouns or pronouns were used.

(4)   Level of play. Any period during which the child showed sustained play activity was classified according to the method described by Lunzer (1959) for measuring 'adaptiveness in the use of play materials' and 'integration of behaviour'. The activities which can be classified on these scales do not cover the whole range of activities the child can be engaged in but deal mainly with the way in which he uses play material, although at the more advanced stages the child's role in relation to other people does assume importance. The scale was

devised for use with normal young children but has been used successfully with a severely subnormal group (Hulme and Lunzer, 1966).

On the scales used to measure the complexity of sentences a child scored 1 if he used only single words and 6 if he used a sentence such as 'Put all the books away bookcase'. The best level of speech produced consisted of sentences such as 'I'm painting', 'I done cupboard' or 'Where's the shoes'.

On the scale measuring level of play, to score 2 a child would have shown no behaviour beyond the level of picking up a toy, examining it superficially and banging it aimlessly. In contrast, the following behaviour scores 8: C is lying with his head on a pillow and M covers him carefully with sheets and blankets. She says she is the doctor and that there is something wrong with C's head. She then sits him on a chair, puts a sheet round his neck, opens his mouth and says either that she is the dentist or that the dentist is needed. A summary of the results is given in Table 4.9.

TABLE 4.9

	Experimental group	*Control group*
No. of words used		
Mean	388	329
Range	71–662	0–624
	(Not significant; $p > .10$)	
No. of different words used		
Mean	74	60
Range	5–138	0–103
	(Not significant; $p > .10$)	
Complexity of sentences (on scale going from 0 to 6+)		
Mean	3.9	3.1
Range	1–6	0–5
	(Not significant; $p > .10$)	
Level of play (on scale going from 0 to 10)		
Mean	6–7	5.4
Range	5–8	2–8
	(Not significant; $p > .10$)	

Although none of these differences reached significance, there was a tendency for those in the experimental group to do better than the children with whom they were matched. Out of a total of 28 comparisons (4 for each child), 18 of the experimental group scores were higher than those of the controls and in only 6 cases did the control child obtain a higher score.

Looking at the group as a whole there was a close link between the children's mental ages and the number of different words they used, the complexity of their sentences and their level of play. This was also true for a small group observed in a junior training centre.

The observations carried out in our group also supported the view that the children used most speech when engaged in activities directly involving other people. On the other hand, they did emerge as having differing personalities and interests, and the importance of treating them as individuals was illustrated. There were also indications that even with an informal regimen there was a necessity for the teacher to take an active part in guiding the children's steps along new lines so that they made good use of all the opportunities available.

The lower grade group

Information on the achievements and general behaviour of the lower grade children was obtained from the nursing staff and also by observing them individually and in the company of people they knew. As far as possible information was collected from more than one source for each area studied.

First set of observations on lower grade group

The material was grouped under three headings: (1) response to speech; (2) responsiveness to adults; and (3) general emotional adjustment. The 11 pairs of children were studied annually.

(1 and 2) *Response to speech and responsiveness to adults.* — A comparison of results for 1964 and 1967 showed, firstly, that on 51 per cent of the scores there was no change and, secondly, that the pattern of change (that is, the number of children moving in a positive or negative direction) was similar for both groups.

(3) *General emotional adjustment.* — Over the 3-year period a number of children remained at the top of the scales covering this area; that is, they were usually happy and cried only under provocation, they were not aggressive unless hit and very rarely had severe temper tantrums or screaming attacks. In the remainder of the cases the majority of changes taking place amongst the experimental group were in a positive direction and amongst the control group in a negative direction (χ^2 significant at .05 level).

This suggests that lower grade children in the experimental group were happier and more settled than their controls even though their general attainments remained limited.

Second set of observations on lower grade group

A further series of observations was made on the experimental ward alone and some of the results are included here as they illustrate again both the extremely low level of functioning of the children and the limited amount of change which takes place.

Eight children (only 1 of whom had a brief trial in school) were studied in a play situation for a total of an hour each. Results are given for September 1964 and compared with those of 2 years later. Initially the ages ranged from 4 years 10 months to 8 years 2 months; 5 could walk independently, and 1 with help; all could sit unaided.

Response to adults. — In 1964, only 1 of the children showed an active positive response to being approached by an adult; 4 showed some positive response, although this might only take the form of watching or taking toys offered; 3 ignored or avoided approaches made to them. In 1966, 4 fell in the first category and 2 in each of the others.

In 1964, 2 children made repeated attempts which seemed to be directed towards gaining the attention of adults, 3 made an attempt to draw attention to themselves although not very persistently and 3 made no attempt to initiate contacts with adults. In 1967, 3 made repeated attempts to initiate contact, 1 made isolated attempts and 4 made no attempt at all.

Response to other children. — The contact between the children was very limited. In 1964, none of the children showed an active interest in the others; 5 watched or made some tentative contact; 3 showed ignoring or avoiding reactions. In 1967, 2 showed an active interest; 2 showed brief interest and 4 ignored or avoided others.

Use of play material. — In 1964, 5 of the children showed no play beyond the level of simple repetitive activities such as banging and shaking and, of these, 2 mainly sucked toys or incorporated them into their manneristic movements. One was able to use two things together and 2 children carried out more complex activities such as building bricks or fitting things in and out of each other. In 1967, 6 children did not spontaneously go beyond the level of banging or shaking; 1 used two things together and 1 used several things.

Vocalizations. — Many of the children's vocalizations were not true speech sounds such as vowels or single or double syllables but consisted of repeated shrieking or singing noises. In 1964, 6 children made no attempt to communicate by using sound but 1 was heard to use sounds to register protest and 1 to attract attention. In 1967, 3 of these 8 children used sounds in some attempt to communicate, chiefly in order to attract attention.

Taking the results as a whole, 3 of the children showed more positive than negative changes, and 3 more negative than positive. Over half their scores remained the same on both occasions.

Woodward and Stern (1963) found a relationship between the subdivisions of the sensorimotor stage and the development of severely subnormal children in a variety of areas. These included speech development, verbal comprehension and social response. When the present data were examined in a similar way, it was found that there was a close relationship between Piaget stages and response to speech, attempts to communicate and speech used and understood. The relationship was not so close with general emotional adjustment or with the child showing an interest in other people (as opposed to actively trying to attract their attention).

The reasons for the lack of progress in this group may not be difficult to find. Throughout the hospital the children are continually kept under review and it is unlikely that any child is under-functioning so grossly as to appear untrainable when he is capable of making a good response. It is worth noting that many children, although they were functioning at a low level on admission, did come from good home environments. It seems reasonable to suggest that in the majority of cases poor attainments are largely the result of lack of ability rather than lack of stimulation.

SELF-HELP SKILLS

One of the aims of the experiment was to increase the children's independence in skills essential for daily living, the 'self-help skills'. These were:

(1) locomotor skills;
(2) feeding skills;
(3) dressing and washing skills; and
(4) toilet training skills.

It is felt that independence or partial independence for self-help is important for all handicapped children. Independence helps children to be socially acceptable, increases their self-respect and the respect of other people for them. In the long term, independence lessens the burden of nursing or parental care although, in the short term, it may increase the work of the adults caring for the child; that is, it is often quicker to dress a child than to teach him to dress himself.

Progress for self-help was assessed by means of four scales, covering the areas mentioned above, which were derived from published scales of normal child development. The scales of normal development used were those of Griffiths (1954) and Gesell and Amatruda (1947). This meant that scores on each scale could be expressed in terms of an equivalent age; that is, the age at which the average normal child achieved the particular skill.

The children in the experimental group and the control group were assessed on these scales at the beginning of the experiment in January 1964 and annually until January 1967. Although it was not possible to match the children of each group on these scales, there was very little difference between the two groups at the beginning of the experiment.

RESULTS

(1)   The experimental children made significantly more progress than the control group (χ^2 significant at .01 level).

(2)   The 6 lower grade children in the experimental group made slightly less progress than the 6 lower grade children in the control group, but this was not significant and very little progress was made by any of the lower grade children in either group.

(3)   The attainments of both groups at the end of the experiment were such that 6 experimental children and 4 of the controls were rated as virtually independent for self-help. This meant that they could run, jump and manage stairs, dress and bath themselves, use a knife and fork and care for themselves at the toilet.

There were 8 experimental children and 10 controls who were partially and usefully independent. They were independent for locomotor skills, in feeding they could feed themselves with a spoon and cup and some could do more, in dressing they could help usefully and on the toilet training scale they were all clean and dry during the day and the majority were beginning to care for themselves. The remaining 6 children in both groups, who were the lower grade children, were still totally dependent on all scales except that 4 experimental children and 3 controls could walk; however, they could walk at the beginning of the experiment.

(4)   These self-help scales had a ceiling of 5 years. It was significant that all the trainable children in both the experimental and the control groups who had mental ages of 2 years or more had achievement ages on these scales at a level ahead of their mental ages; in fact, they had made more progress than one might have expected in learning to be independent. Other workers (Marshall, 1967) have found that trainable severely subnormal children can achieve a surprisingly high standard of personal independence and our findings in both groups support this.

TEACHING

Assessments were made every year and results were fed back to the staff in two ways. Firstly, by means of a wall chart which showed what each child was doing and suggesting what the next step should be; these charts were available to both teaching and nursing staff. Secondly, when the annual assessments of individual children were made, the results were discussed at the weekly meetings and future plans were discussed by everyone concerned. These meetings were minuted and although minutes were not used to assess the success of the plan, this could in fact be done. The nursing staff found the wall charts were particularly useful for junior staff. The actual training of the children was carried out by the teaching and nursing staff.

DISCUSSIONS AND RECOMMENDATIONS

The children seemed to fall into two groups: the school children, imbeciles, who made progress in self-help skills, and the heavily handicapped idiot children who changed very little.

It was felt that some method of annual assessment and discussion was useful, particularly with the brighter children. It pin-pointed areas in which they needed help and also those in which progress had been made, and this was encouraging for the staff. It also ensured that everyone working with the children knew what stage they were at and what was the plan for the future.

The very severely handicapped, idiot children seemed to present a different problem. In our experiment they made practically no progress, which makes one wonder whether even partial independence is an important aim for this group. This requires further research using different methods.

Summary and Discussion

An account has been given of an attempt to modify the environment of 20 children living in a ward for the severely subnormal in a comprehensive children's hospital. The work was carried out within the ordinary framework of the shift system and without increasing the staffing ratio. Although continuity of contact was established to only a limited degree, it was possible to increase the amount of stimulation the children received and to introduce a more 'individualized' regimen.

The brighter children (the imbecile group) clearly benefited from the changes in the pattern of care, as is illustrated by their progress compared with a matched group living in other wards. Had the adults been more permanent, even greater changes might have resulted.

The position with regard to the lower grade children was rather different. The experimental group made slightly more progress than the control group, but the most striking feature was the limited amount of change which took place. This applied in all areas, including self-help. It was felt that in general this group was of such low ability that marked changes could not reasonably be expected. Any improvements might be centred around their emotional adjustment and there was some evidence that the experimental group did better in this area than their controls.

In view of the limited progress of these children, the usefulness of giving them toys and of attempting to stimulate them may be questioned. However, most of them were capable of responding at a simple level and the humane approach would be to provide such stimulation as they can use. This can be looked at in the same way as is the excellent physical care they already receive. It is of particular importance that the younger children be helped and encouraged, as it is not always easy to make reliable predictions about their future development.

Looking at the over-all picture, one of the most pressing needs which emerged was for continuity of contact with adults. Where this is not possible, every effort should be made to pass on information about the children and to discuss their management so that at least the pattern of care is continuous. We were fortunate in that the groups in the experiment contained only 20 children. To obtain individualized handling in a 60-bedded ward would have been very difficult; where such units exist, some subdivision seems essential.

We are fully conscious of the halo effect resulting from the increased interest shown by ourselves and other members of the hospital team. However, this does not detract from the fact that it was possible to bring about considerable changes within the limitations imposed by the frequent changes of staff, by the staff/ child ratio and the general physical environment.

Perhaps the most important factor in determining whether or not a high standard of care is achieved is the extent to which the principles we have laid down are genuinely accepted both by those people directly involved in the day-to-day care of the children and by the administration as a whole.

There is a need to look further at the problems of providing for the lower grade children. As community care and hostel provisions increase, this group will make up an increasingly large percentage of the hospital population. It may be that some at least could be cared for in small units attached to general hospitals, as suggested by Tizard (1960), rather than being grouped together in large institutions.

Lower grade children who are active and show disturbed behaviour present special problems and we need to build up a body of knowledge about them in the way which has already been done for the brighter ones.

Recent work in the U.S.A. suggests that Skinnerian techniques may offer a solution, but at present this has been carried out mainly with groups whose potential is at least in the imbecile rather than the idiot range.

Handling severely retarded children well is a highly skilled task and it is

158

important that staff be properly trained. We feel that there is room in the present system for greater emphasis on child development, on ways of meeting the children's emotional needs, of stimulating and occupying them and of making good use of play material, In addition, it can be very demanding for adults to work with children who make little response and limited progress, and we should also be looking for ways to make this difficult work as rewarding as possible.

At present, recruiting figures are lower in subnormality than in all other branches of nursing. However, increasing emphasis is being placed on the training and education of the patient. It is becoming recognized that learning is an ongoing process, and nurses as well as teachers must have some knowledge of teaching techniques.

The General Nursing Council is also encouraging hospitals to allow student nurses to spend time in day training centres where they can gain experience of less handicapped patients. This could be extended to include periods in residential homes for normal children, but, with present staff shortages, any such arrangements must be almost impossible for the majority of hospitals to arrange.

Put Away, by Dr. Pauline Morris (1969), has been published since our experiment ended. As this is a sociological study of institutions for the mentally retarded, it is extremely relevant to our work and we would like to discuss her findings in some detail.

(1)   Dr. Morris criticizes subnormality hospitals because their objectives are not clear and therefore treatment is uniform and not geared to individual patients. In answer to this criticism we defined some of our objectives by the scales we used to assess the children and measure progress. We were, in fact, using scales similar to those used by Gunzburg (1968) and in a similar way. We devised our own measures because Gunzburg's primary progress assessment chart was not available when the experiment started. Our measures could be improved and extended but we suggest that this is one way of defining objectives and checking on progress.

(2)   Another criticism made by Dr. Morris is a lack of communication and lack of integration with the community. We tried to overcome the difficulty of communication by regular ward meetings which included periodic discussions of the children's progress with everyone concerned. We think that 'communication' does depend on having someone responsible for organizing the work; in our case it was the psychologists who were responsible for the experiment. We tried to meet Dr. Morris's point about the need for integration in the community by the involvement of parents and voluntary workers in the ways we have described.

(3)   Dr. Morris suggests that heterogeneous groups of patients are desirable whereas in subnormality hospitals they tend to be grouped homogeneously. We had the impression that our group was too heterogeneous, that we had too many

159

lower grade, idiot children who tended to hold back the progress of the imbecile children because, as we have pointed out, they had different needs. However, this is a question which requires further investigation.

(4)   Dr. Morris has criticized the poor physical conditions – 'positively Dickensian' – in some subnormality hospitals. Although we had only 20 children in the ward whereas 'over one-third of the patients sleep in dormitories of sixty or more', we feel that we only partially succeeded in making the ward comfortable and homelike.

(5)   Dr. Morris also criticized one hospital's psychology department for carrying out empirical research lacking in scientific validity. Our research is open to this criticism in that the psychologists responsible for planning the ward programme also carried out the assessments and evaluated the results. We were forced to do this because we did not have facilities for blind assessments.

(6)   Finally, Dr. Morris has suggested that there is a need for social therapists to train and educate severely subnormal patients. We are suggesting that as an alternative interim method it should be possible to improve conditions in hospital using the present staff in the way we have described.

ACKNOWLEDGEMENTS

We should like to thank the many people who have helped to make this experiment a success. Our special thanks go to Professor Jack Tizard and Mrs. Elinor Goldschmied for their advice and support and to all the people at the hospital, particularly Miss V. Hopkins, Sister B. Lunn, Dr. G. Woods, Dr. E. Donoghue, Miss D. Jones (Matron), and Mr. R. Durrant (Deputy Group Secretary). We should also like to thank Mrs. E. Elliott who typed our manuscript.

Appendix: Details of the Children's Activities

The continuity between ward and school is illustrated in this description of the children's activities, although as a greater number of observations were carried out in school, the emphasis may be found to be more in this direction.

We should like to thank the teacher and the nursing staff for helping us to put this material together by discussing the children in great detail.

SAND

The majority of the group made good use of the sand tray in the class-room and at least half were very interested in it. It seemed particularly valuable both in that it gave rise to some of the most complex play shown by the younger children and in that it brought the children together. Some of the earliest signs of children interacting and imitating each other were seen around the sand. The children would not always allow the adult to show them what to do, but a good deal of speech could be stimulated by asking them about their work.

Eating the sand or throwing it for fun was a problem until the group became used to having it available. It is necessary to have a cover which can easily be put on if throwing persists or if for any special reason the children are not to play with the sand. We found a simple cotton cover, which could be tied with tapes round the legs of the tray, to be quite adequate. The children learned to look after the sand and some began to learn to sweep up without help.

If the best use is to be made of the sand, there should be sufficient in stock so that it can always be available. It was found that rubber tools and moulds were the best because they last longest, are easier to keep clean and, most important, are safe to use. The sand must be kept damp and, as it gets smelly, must be sprinkled with disinfectant nearly every day.

There was also sand in the adventure playground and this was very popular with the more advanced of the pre-school children as well as with the school group. Many of the children occupied themselves but others needed help even to handle it. Throwing was a problem and, in addition to throwing the sand, the children tossed spades and other toys over the fence and on to the roof. There was no cover for the sand pit because this would have been too cumbersome to manage; instead we concentrated on teaching the children not to throw. Since children with mental ages of under 2 may take many years to learn this, a sand pit may not be suitable for all wards. Sand was also used indoors but this happened infrequently because it tended to be a very messy activity and there was sand available outside and in the school.

MUSIC

Many of the children derived a good deal of pleasure from music; it helped in teaching some of the more disturbed children to overcome their tempers and aggressive behaviour and it also helped very noticeably one of the lower grade children with his speech.

It is very important that as much music as possible be presented at first hand. As the children became musically more sophisticated, they enjoyed listening to records but this probably represented a relatively advanced stage. Either a piano or a tambourine makes a good accompaniment to singing or 'band'. The children can be drawn together, the rhythm emphasized and the pace suited to the group. Although some parts of the day must be organized, it was an advantage to be able to have singing and dancing whenever it was felt that the children would be most receptive to it. We found it important to keep songs simple and as personal and related to everyday things as possible. It was equally important to avoid lengthy group repetition with all of the children sitting round whether they were interested or not. It was decided to give them free access to the piano unless it was being misused and after a fairly short time they learned to look after it well. In this way it was revealed that one child possessed remarkable musical ability which it has since been possible to develop.

'Band' is probably best introduced as a fairly formal activity because care must be taken of the instruments and the children need to be helped to concentrate. With a disturbed group, bells make a good introduction to musical instruments. This is one time when a small group, perhaps of 5 or 6 children, is particularly desirable and an extra adult who can take another activity with the rest of the group would be very useful. As the teachers will vary among themselves in the extent to which they can provide 'music' for the children this might be an area for specialization.

We were fortunate in that one of the teacher's assistants could play the viola and a friend brought her guitar to play for the group. The children were very interested to see and hear these instruments and there might be a role for a visitor who would bring an instrument to play to selected groups of children.

The children enjoyed listening to the record player in the ward, but this was kept as a special activity and not just part of the daily routine. The school children sang and danced to the music, but only 2 of the pre-school group showed any real interest.

WATER PLAY

Water play was used very little in the classrooms because the water tray was not really big enough for the boisterous movements of the children, particularly the bigger ones. Water play would have been possible and enjoyable if most of the group had been small children. Similar problems were encountered in the ward when a water tray was used. The children enjoyed playing with the water at bathtime but there was not much time to spend on this.

The children were able to learn something about the properties and limitations of water when they bathed the doll or helped to wash up, but it seemed as if they needed a pool where their whole bodies could enjoy the experience. This was met to a large extent by the weekly visits to the swimming pool which most of the children enjoyed very much. Besides 'swimming' they had an opportunity to play with toys and learned to understand the properties of water. The ideal situation is for them to be able to take the water-play toys into a little swimming pool or in an out-of-doors paddling pool in the summer.

BOOKS

An interest in books and pictures is very important in relation to speech development, but many books are unsuitable because the pictures are unclear and the subject matter quite unrelated to the children's experience. A set of *Conversation Pictures* published by Schofield and Sons, which deals with everyday activities in the home, is particularly recommended. During the 3 years the extent to which the children could sit with a book and concentrate increased markedly. A lot of speech arose in this situation both between the children and adults and between the children themselves.

It is necessary to set high standards for looking after books, but at the same time it is important to have them freely available. Because some of the children tended to tear and throw them a lot, particularly in the initial stages, books were divided into those which were allowed out only under supervision and those which were always on the shelf. Towards the end of the experiment the behaviour of most of the children had improved and many of them could be trusted with the 'best' books without close supervision. The books to which the children always had access were specially made so that they would stand up to rough wear. Parents and friends are often willing to help but need to be given some idea of the sort of pictures to choose and how to make something really strong and long-lasting. Tearing or cutting out from magazines was not encouraged as the aim was to teach the children a respect for books. It was not felt that magazines had a great contribution to make as the pages were often too thin for the children to turn and the pictures uninteresting or too sophisticated. Rag books do not teach the real nature and use of a book. It proved to be very difficult to keep books intact in the ward as many of the pre-school children, too, were at the tearing stage and at least some of them showed no real awareness that they were doing something wrong.

To obtain the most benefit from books, children need a special protected place in which to look at them. Towards the end of the experiment we found that it was a great advantage to have a small carpeted area in the classroom with a bookcase and two easy chairs. The children made good use of this, and a comfortable and relatively sheltered area helped to produce a good atmosphere in the room.

IMAGINATIVE PLAY

Initially very few imaginative activities were seen in our group and it was only during the last 6 months that imaginative play occurred nearly every day in school. Items of play still lasted for only a short time, however; the children tended to switch roles often and easily and sequences were not followed through in a highly integrated manner.

Because we know that imaginative play has an important role both in language development and in helping the child to mature socially and emotionally, a good deal of emphasis was placed on encouraging it. An important part of this was to provide outings and other new activities which would increase the children's experiences and give them something to draw on. The actual play material

163

included a Wendy house (reinforced and fixed to the floor), dressing-up clothes, floor bricks, dolls, a doll's cot and pram, furniture for the house, an iron and ironing board and a teapot. Dressing-up clothes, dolls and bricks were all available in the ward as well. All of these items needed to be as freely accessible as possible if full use was to be made of them, but we found it necessary to remove toys when they were being misused and some of the more fragile toys could only be used under some degree of supervision.

However carefully they were chosen, many of the toys mentioned above tended to be damaged easily and it would have been useful if a handy-man could have carried out minor repairs on the spot.

PAINTING

Children at all levels enjoyed painting a good deal, although not all had the idea of creating shape and form. There were relatively few problems caused by the paint being deliberately misused, but those with poor motor co-ordination often knocked the paint over by accident. If there were several in the group who could not be left alone in the room for a short time and if some needed a lot of help to clean themselves up, two adults were needed. Those who did not present any management problems needed encouragement to talk about their work and they had to learn not to 'paint out' what they had done.

As we had hoped, they learned to take pride in their work and learned relatively quickly to look after the paintings when they were put on the wall. If there was sufficient space, they were put at eye level and this should be borne in mind when considering the position of display boards. It was found that good quality paper was necessary because thinner paper tore very easily, often before the paintings were finished. Stocks of paint and paper needed replenishing frequently.

TABLE APPARATUS

A variety of table apparatus was used; plenty of easily accessible cupboard space was required as the aim was for the children to choose their own material. For many groups, cupboards with doors which can be locked if necessary are preferable to open shelves, but some toys should always be available. These can be kept on the window sills and cupboard tops when the room is tidied, but should not be put away completely.

It was hoped that the children's manipulative skills would increase and also that they would learn to sit and concentrate and to persist when they met difficulties. It was intended that they should learn to choose their own equipment and be responsible for putting it away. On the whole they did learn to do these things, but the lower grade children needed stricter supervision and more help in all areas. The role of the adult was very important in helping the child to overcome frustration, to increase his attention span and to move on to new things.

A good stock of equipment graded according to the children's level was necessary. Some children tended to lose interest if required to do the same thing again and again, and others who were content to stay with familiar pieces of apparatus needed a lot of encouragement and something which took their eye, before they moved on to something new and more advanced.

On the whole, table apparatus did not seem very useful for stimulating social interaction between the children, but the bricks (which in fact were mainly used on the floor) did attract more than one child at a time, stimulated imitation and gave rise to a lot of imaginative play.

Cupboards make useful room dividers but we found that if they were to provide a protected corner for working in, more space was needed than would be required for a nursery school group. Our children were bigger and often tended to be clumsy so that they knocked things over very easily. They also demanded more help from the adult and there had to be room for her to move amongst them. It would be useful if this could be experimented with in other classes.

A supply of equipment similar to that used in the school was kept in the ward and used chiefly at week-ends or when the school girls came in the evening. It is discussed more fully in the section on 'Toys in the ward'.

SCISSORS

We had not thought of introducing scissors to any extent, but one of the female adult patients who helped in the classroom was very interested in cutting out. Once one or two of the older children became interested, the others followed suit. Some of the children took a long time to learn to use them. The scissors were quite sharp and this is necessary if the children are to learn to cut properly. We found that as long as a few simple rules were obeyed they did not represent any real problem. In the ward, scissors were used in Sister's office, but a few of the children were allowed to fetch them if they asked for them.

GROSS MOTOR ACTIVITIES

The children enjoyed using the swings and climbing equipment in the playground and school hall and made good use of the large floor apparatus in the classroom. The group was sometimes split so that some children remained behind in the classroom to concentrate on a particular activity while the others went outside. Using the classroom apparatus helped the children to learn about taking turns and was an activity in which most of them wanted to join if one child started a game.

165

Several of the children had great difficulty in controlling their movements and these were probably helped more by the adventure playground than by anything else. After using the playground it was noticed that their skill in swinging, balancing and climbing improved a good deal.

This area might provide further opportunities for specialization amongst the staff.

SWIMMING POOL AND THE TEA-SHOP

Two of the children's favourite activities were going to the tea-shop in the Friends' Centre and to the swimming pool. Both of these were in the hospital grounds. Although all of them went on the same afternoon, they split into two groups with a teacher in each, one leaving earlier than the other. In the pool they were helped and encouraged by the physiotherapist and because of this swimming became a great joy to most of them. Some were able to copy the races they had seen on television. One child was rather frightened of the water and needed to be introduced to it very gradually. It is important that such information is passed on if a different person from usual is responsible for the children.

Tea in the Friends' Centre was enjoyable but also valuable in that it helped the children to learn to behave in a socially acceptable way and it was a good preparation for visits outside the hospital, including trips home. The children found it much easier to accept new experiences if they were first introduced in familiar surroundings.

OUTINGS OUTSIDE THE HOSPITAL

Many of the children had not had much experience of the world outside the hospital and they took some time to adjust to it and to learn how to behave.

They enjoyed all forms of outing but, if the aim is to help them to gain experience, isolated group outings have limited value. It is most important that they should be able to join in actively, although at first they will need a lot of support and supervision. It is not uncommon for children to have temper tantrums and to create a great disturbance because they are very nervous and anxious in a new situation.

Outings from the school were never very frequent or regular and because of this were not satisfactory. On these outings several classes went out in the coach and, if it was fine, a group got out and either played or went to the shops. It was possible to take only very few children into a shop at once as they wanted to touch everything and there was no time to do more than buy sweets and come out again. The children were destructive and aggressive if they could not get what they wanted and were ambivalent towards dogs, wanting to approach them and then being frightened or excited, so that they tended to frighten the animals.

Because we felt that outings outside the hospital had a very important role to play, we decided to organize some of our own. It was possible for the hospital to arrange transport for special occasions, but this could not be provided on a regular basis and, in addition, might mean depriving the rest of the school of a trip out. Initially, our outings were within walking distance but later we went further afield, the staff using their own cars to transport the children. This was not very time consuming for the drivers, as the group could be transported and collected again in an hour or so.

Two adults would certainly be needed with 9 or 10 children and more with a young or disturbed group. Again, aunties and regular voluntary helpers can play a very important role. It was found, however, that too many helpers, particularly if they were strangers, could cause difficulties. For example, the children may behave badly and keep wanting to change the person with whom they are walking. A push-chair was usually taken and the big pram was useful if the walk was a long one or a child was likely to be dirty. The excitement of an outing regularly caused an 'accident' in one child who was otherwise toilet trained.

The outings were made as varied as possible but usually included shopping or going to a tea-shop in one of the parks. We went shopping and to watch the trains, to the park or to visit the tea-shop. On one occasion we saw some cows at very close quarters. Small groups went on a train. At first the children were only used to buying sweets, but later were introduced to cake, ice-cream, fruit and toys as well. They found fruit difficult to accept, but often chose it later. They also bought the cake and other things when there was to be a birthday party. One day the children were able to look in the hairdresser's window and see people having their hair done and were able to go into the shoe repairer's and see the man mending the shoes. The children's reactions to 'shopping' changed a good deal. They were much calmer and less aggressive and more able to choose what they wanted. The adult may, of course, engineer which shops they go into and can help them to limit their choice to a few things. They were able to understand that unless it was a special occasion they could buy only one thing and accepted the idea that if they had sweets they could not have a toy or ice-cream as well. In general, the outings which were very hectic at first became much more pleasurable.

We found the shopkeepers all very friendly and helpful, but the children were sometimes puzzled when strangers did not understand what they were saying.

The children's first experience of the tea-shop was their weekly visit to the Friends' Centre in the hospital. When they were sufficiently well behaved they were taken to the tea-shops in parks. It was clear that they needed the experience outside the hospital; the child who could express himself most clearly, showed that he was amazed that tea-shops could be different from each other.

It was found best for dogs and the children to be quite separate from each other. Sometimes the children sat outside on the grass, but it was found that they behaved much better if they sat up to the table.

The children went on a number of visits to private houses and, although they were out of doors most of the time, they went inside to look around. They were particularly interested in the stairs and the lavatories. When they had to be indoors because of the weather, 4 or 5 were quite enough to manage. The older children improved in that they were calmer and were quite good at looking after people's things, but the younger ones needed very close supervision.

Besides group outings, many children were taken out by the staff and friends as well as by their own parents. The children usually enjoyed these trips a good deal although they got more out of them if they knew the people they were with, particularly if the things they were going to do were strange to them.

The best outing of all was when Sister took a group on a caravan holiday, although the credit here must go to Sister and not to the 'experiment'. In general, the children's behaviour improved as they became familiar with situations; this emphasizes the importance of their trips outside the hospital being frequent and regular.

EXTRA EXPERIENCES

Right from the beginning it was realized that the children's experiences were very limited and that they knew very little of the day-to-day events which occur in the home. We tried to introduce as many activities as possible which would help to fill this gap. A knowledge of the world around them is very important if the children are to mature socially and play useful roles in whatever environment they find themselves as adults. While they were eager for new things, in practice they often found them very difficult to accept.

Cooking

The children had very little experience of food being prepared because most of their meals arrived from a central kitchen. Important steps towards overcoming this were made in the ward, where they were encouraged to help to prepare their drinks at night and to make sandwiches, jelly and scrambled eggs for tea. All but 2 of the 'full-time' school children were able to take a turn and 2 of them started to lay the trolley by themselves. They enjoyed helping with the washing up, but were only allowed to do this one at a time. It seems important that the brighter children should lèarn to avoid everyday danger such as things being too hot and they cannot do this if they are protected entirely. Which children are allowed into the kitchen must, of course, depend on the discretion of the sister or charge nurse.

We had hoped to have an oven in the school so that the children could see the preparation of food from the beginning, but this was not installed in time. 'Cooking' in the classroom had to be limited to things which did not need heating. One day it was possible to arrange for some cakes to be mixed in the morning and baked during the lunch hour, but this was not very satisfactory as it was not possible to be certain that a link had been established between the uncooked cakes and the finished product. More suitable things were fruit, 'whips', decorating cakes and making fruit drinks.

Alternative activities had to be available because, although nearly everyone joined in at some stage, all of the children's interests were not maintained all of the time. Two people were needed for 'cooking' unless the group was a very small or very stable one.

Fruit

Fruit given to the children in the ward tended to be cut up and it emerged that the children did not really know how to eat fresh oranges, apples and bananas. For this reason Wednesday became 'fruit day' in school and the children were given a variety of items to choose from to eat after their milk. Fruit was no longer cut up for the brighter children, but Sister found that several of them still tended not to like hard things and had difficulty in eating an apple. In time they began to choose fruit instead of sweets when they were shopping.

Flowers

The children were shown how to put flowers in water and leave them on the cupboard. Most of the group understood about looking after them and they even survived on the window-ledge in the Wendy house. Pot plants lasted for over a year.

Several of the children were interested in picking wild flowers and bringing them to school or taking them back to Sister. Both mustard and cress and hyacinths were grown in the classroom and the children saw flowers grow in a patch of garden near the ward.

Telephone

The children were familiar with the nursing staff using the telephone and enjoyed having 'conversations' on two telephones in the classroom. We tried toy telephones, but they broke easily and the outsides of ordinary 'phones proved stronger (although they still had to be mended frequently). The children 'talked' to the ward staff or to their parents and aunties and, although the level of the conversation varied with the ability of the child, this proved a valuable means of stimulating imaginative activity. It also helped when the children had been naughty; telling Sister 'me good boy' often seemed to act as a means of saying 'sorry' without losing face. The children talked to some people on the proper telephone, either using the internal hospital 'phone or a call box where they had learned to put the money in.

Decorating the Wendy house

The children were always interested in the various jobs they saw being done around the hospital and they greatly enjoyed helping to paint and paper the Wendy house. Several of them had clearly associated this with what happened when a ward was decorated and brought the experience into their play.

Letters

At Christmas the children made calendars which they then put into an envelope and posted; subsequently several opportunities arose for postcards to be sent and to be received. We feel that the children were familiar with the idea of sending and receiving cards and letters and with post-boxes, but they were probably not really aware of the role of the postman.

Animals

The possibility of keeping a pet was considered, but it was felt that life would be too hard for an animal. An attempt was made to keep some tadpoles in school, but one of the children tipped them down the basin after only a week. It was interesting to see that the two children who were most fascinated by them were the brightest child and the dullest one.

Although the children did not keep a pet, it was possible for them to feed the horse that lived in the field adjoining the playground. One child became particularly fond of him and eventually was able to go alone and could be relied upon to come back when he was called. This child showed a lot of disturbed and aggressive behaviour and his 'friendship' with the horse seemed to help him considerably.

Parties

Parties were held on birthdays and at Christmas at the end of the term, and the children came to expect them. On these occasions they learned the routine of opening parcels and cards and of blowing out the candles and their general behaviour improved a good deal. For example, at the beginning of the experiment when a party was held in school it was necessary to lay the table at the last minute whereas at the end of the experiment it could be laid in the dinner hour because most of the children had learned not to touch it before the proper time. The ability to behave well at a properly laid table is an important one if the child is to go home or on outings. There were more difficulties in the ward because the pre-school group were not so restrained.

170

References

Dinnage, R. and Kellmer Pringle, M. L. (1967). *Residential Care: Facts and Fallacies.* Harlow, Essex: Longmans

Flint, B. M. (1968). *The Child and the Institution.* Toronto: Univ. of Toronto Press

Furneaux, B. (1969). *The Special Child.* Harmondsworth, Middx: Penguin

Gesell, A. and Amatruda, C. (1947). *Development Diagnosis: Normal and Abnormal Child Development.* New York: Harper & Halber; London: Cassell

Griffiths, R. (1954). *The Abilities of Babies.* London: Univ. of London Press

Gunzburg, H. C. (1968). In *Proceedings of the First Congress of the International Association for the Scientific Study of Mental Deficiency, Montpellier, 1967,* p. 236. Ed. by B. W. Richards. Reigate, Surrey: Jackson

Hulme, I. and Lunzer, E. A. (1966). 'Play, language and reasoning in severely subnormal children.' *J. Child Psychol. Psychiat.* 7, 107

Lunzer, E. A. (1959). 'Intellectual development in the play of young children.' *Educ. Rev.* 11, 205

Lyle, J. (1960). 'The effect of an institution environment upon the verbal development of imbecile children. iii: The Brooklands Experiment.' *J. ment. Defic. Res.* 4, 14

Marshall, A. (1967). *The Abilities and Attainments of Children leaving Junior Training Centres.* London: Nat. Assoc. Mental Health

Ministry of Health (1961). *Report of the Sub-Committee of the Training of Staff of Training Centres for the Mentally Retarded.* London: H.M.S.O.

Morris, P. (1969). *Put Away: a Sociological Study of Institutions for the Mentally Retarded.* London: Routledge & Kegan Paul

Piaget, J. (1962). *Play, Dreams and Imitation in Childhood.* London: Routledge & Kegan Paul

Primrose, D. A. (1968). 'Children in the mental deficiency hospitals of Glasgow And Argyll.' *Devl Med. child Neurol.* 10, 366

Raynes, N. V. and King, R. D. (1968). In *Proceedings of the First Congress of the International Association for the Scientific Study of Mental Deficiency, Montpellier, 1967,* p. 637. Ed. by B. W. Richards. Reigate, Surrey: Jackson

Sandler, J. (1955). 'A test of the significance of the difference between means of correlated measures based on a simplification of students t.' *Br. J. Psychol.* 46, 225

Tizard, J. (1960). 'Residential care of mentally handicapped children.' *Br. med. J.* 1, 1041

– (1964). *Community Services for the Mentally Handicapped.* London: Oxford Univ. Press

Williams, G. (1967). *Caring for People: Staffing Residential Homes.* London: Allen & Unwin

Woodward, M. (1959). 'The behaviour of idiots interpreted by Piaget's theory of sensori-motor development.' *Br. J. educ. Psychol.* **29,** 60

— (1963). 'Early experience and behaviour disorders in severely subnormal children.' *Br. J. soc. clin. Psychol.* **2,** 174

— and Stern, D. (1963). 'Developmental patterns of severely subnormal children.' *Br. J. educ. Psychol.* **33,** 10